FOREWORD BY [

The MIRACLE MORNING *for* ADDICTION RECOVERY

Letting Go of Who You've Been for Who You Can Become

Hal Elrod • Anna David • Joe Polish

With Honorée Corder

THE MIRACLE MORNING FOR ADDICTION RECOVERY

Hal Elrod, Anna David & Joe Polish
with Honorée Corder

Interior Design: Christina Gorchos, 3CsBooks.com

Paperback ISBN: 978-1-942589-25-9
E book IBSN: 978-1-942589-26-6

DEDICATIONS

Hal

This book is dedicated to the people who mean more to me than anything in the world—my family. Mom. Dad. My sister, Hayley. My wife, Ursula, and our two children—Sophie and Halsten. I love you all more than I can put into words!

This book is also in loving memory of my sister, Amery Kristine Elrod.

Anna and Joe

For all the addicts out there, who have found a solution or are still looking for one. Life can always get better. And mornings are the best place to start.

CONTENTS

SECTION I: The Miracle Morning + Life S.A.V.E.R.S.

The case for mornings and why they are critically important to an addict's success (and what happens when you don't take advantage of them).

Even if you've never been a morning person, you're about to discover the simplest and most effective way to overcome the challenge of waking up early, conquer the snooze button, and maximize your mornings.

Harness the life-changing power of the most effective, proven personal development practices known to man, which are guaranteed to save you from missing out on the levels of success (in every area of your life) that you truly want and deserve.

SECTION II: The Not-So-Obvious Recovery Principles

Discover why who you're becoming is significantly more important than what you say and do each day and precisely how to lead yourself to the next level, so that you can take your success to the next level (because it only happens in that order).

When it comes to recovery, managing your energy is significantly more important than managing your time. Discover how to strategically engineer your life to sustain extraordinary levels of physical, mental, and emotional energy.

Discover how to increase your productivity and get more done, by developing your ability to consistently prioritize, plan, and maintain unwavering focus in regard to your highest priorities, regardless of outside forces and distractions.

SECTION III: Level 10 Recovery Skills

A SPECIAL INVITATION FROM HAL

Readers and practitioners of *The Miracle Morning* have co-created an extraordinary community consisting of over 200,000 like-minded individuals from around the world who wake up each day *with purpose* and dedicate time to fulfilling the unlimited potential that is within all of us, while helping others to do the same.

As author of *The Miracle Morning*, I felt that I had a responsibility to create an online community where readers could come together to connect, get encouragement, share best practices, support one another, discuss the book, post videos, find an accountability partner, and even swap smoothie recipes and exercise routines.

However, I honestly had no idea that The Miracle Morning Community would become one of the most positive, engaged, and supportive online communities in the world, but it has. I'm constantly astounded by the caliber and the character of our members, which presently includes people from over seventy countries and is growing daily.

Just go to **www.MyTMMCommunity.com** and request to join The Miracle Morning Community on Facebook. You'll immediately be able to connect with 130,000+ people who are already practicing TMM. While you'll find many who are just beginning their Miracle Morning journey, you'll find even more who have been at it for years and will happily share advice, support, and guidance to accelerate your success.

I moderate the Community and check in regularly, so I look forward to seeing you there! If you'd like to connect with me personally on social media, just follow **@HalElrod** on Twitter and **Facebook.com/YoPalHal** on Facebook. Let's connect soon!

FOREWORD

Addiction is a serious disease, and it sounds glib to say that something as simple as attending to your mornings can somehow magically influence the course of recovery.

But the fact is that it is no less magical than an aphorism to which we are all deeply attached because of its efficacy: One Day at a Time. Of course, focusing on one day at a time can have very personal and diverse meaning, but the reality is that one day at a time must be attended through one morning at a time.

It is well known that the daily hormonal fluctuations are profoundly affected by light and time we awaken. We are hormonally different in the morning hours than later in the day. History is replete with observations about the importance of morning and its influence on the rest of our day. This is not fiction but rather biological as well as a pragmatic reality, and it needs to be acknowledged and nurtured.

Addicts lose track of how to live, and those of us treating addicts often forget the importance of attending to the basics that then become the scaffolding for a rich and flourishing recovery. What drew me into the field of addiction treatment was watching extraordinary people regain a thriving existence.

This was something in which I wished to participate: human flourishing.

When happiness experts are queried about what one thing an individual can do to contribute to happiness, the answer is often simply to make your bed. It makes some sense intuitively that, in addition to attending to a fellowship and a recovery process involving close relationships with fellow addicts, the structure and conduct of the day is a critical ingredient of recovery.

Here you will find a blueprint for, well, getting started. And that is the first step in every day, one day at a time.

—Dr. Drew Pinsky

Dr. Drew Pinsky is Board Certified in Internal Medicine and Addiction Medicine. He is the host of *Dr. Drew on Call* (HLN), *Celebrity Rehab with Dr. Drew*, *Loveline* radio show and numerous podcasts, as well as the *New York Times* best-selling author of *The Mirror Effect: How Celebrity Narcissism is Seducing America* (Harper-Collins) and *Cracked: Putting Broken Lives Together Again* (Harper-Collins).

A NOTE FROM ANNA DAVID

MY MIRACLE MORNING

"Live life like it's rigged in your favor"
—RUMI

Mornings used to be…well, often a time I would miss altogether. It can be challenging to rise before noon, after all, if you've stayed up all night, high as a kite the evening before, long enough to hear the birds chirp. Mornings were to be avoided, slept through, and ignored. Mornings were when basic people, those who subscribed to all the world's ridiculous norms, went to work.

Imagine my surprise, then, when I found recovery and discovered that I not only love mornings, but also that I am a full-fledged morning person. My former party girl self would be horrified to discover that my natural body clock has me asleep by about 10 p.m. and up before 7 a.m. That's a good thing, by the way; horrifying my former party girl self means I'm doing something right.

Mornings Are a Big Topic for Those in Recovery

One of the first suggestions I got from my outpatient rehab was that I should make my bed first thing in the morning, since it showed both a determination to get out of it as well as a commitment to being a responsible person for the day. Done! Being able to cross an item of a to-do list in roughly twenty seconds does wonders for a person's dopamine.

This is also when I learned to pray. The process started like this: my sponsor took me through the twelve steps and when we got to the one that involved praying, I explained to her that there was no way I could get on my knees and talk to God.

"I'm Jewish," I explained.

She smiled. "So am I," she answered.

I probably made another excuse.

Then she said, "I get how uncomfortable this is at first. Why don't you drop your keys on the ground next to your bed, and when you kneel down to get them, talk to God?"

I actually did that.

And I learned that getting down on my knees and praying wasn't the creepy experience I'd imagined it would be.

Surprisingly, it felt comforting. And so, I've continued to do it every morning. Without having to drop my keys.

But Then I Went Beyond Bed–Making and Prayer

For the first five years of sobriety, I went to a 7:30 a.m. 12-step meeting Monday through Friday. Then, one night about twelve years ago, a friend from the program invited me to a lecture by a Vedic Meditation teacher (Vedic Meditation is an offshoot of Transcendental Meditation and involves repeatedly thinking a mantra).

Despite the fact that I'd long said I was someone who simply could not meditate—I often told people that my mind was simply too busy—I ended up receiving my mantra that very night.

To my utter shock, I committed to the process of meditating every morning and evening for 20 minutes. And I'll never forget what the meditation teacher who gave the talk that night, Thom Knoles, said when people started chiming in about how there was no way they could spare 20 minutes every morning.

"If you can't spare 20 minutes in the morning to do something that will radically improve your life," he said with the utmost seriousness, "you need to change your life."

I Took It a Step Further

About a year into my 20-minute morning meditation routine, I added something else: reading a page of spiritual literature before closing my eyes and thinking my mantra. This literature has ranged over the years—for a while I would read a page out of Melodie Beattie's *The Language of Letting Go*, and then I went through a phase of reading different 12-step One Day at a Time books. Now, I subscribe to meditation teacher Jeff Kober's daily newsletter, and so I read that every morning pre-meditation.

Discovering *The Miracle Morning* in the past year has taken my morning routine, as they say in *This is Spinal Tap*, to eleven. Because I tend to exercise later in the day, the importance of getting my blood pumping first thing had never occurred to me. And I'd never been much of an affirmations person, always imagining myself standing in front of the mirror, saying I loved myself and feeling silly. And journal writing, for me, was limited to 12-step work and times when I was feeling especially angsty.

But reading *The Miracle Morning* changed that. I built on the morning routine I already had—a process I detail later in the book. And these slight tweaks somehow changed everything—my career, relationships and, most importantly, how I feel about myself.

Why Mornings Are Important for Those in Recovery

Although there are many definitions for "addict," mine is someone who feels things so deeply that he or she will do anything possible to change a feeling—even if changing that feeling could mean dying. I'm not even sure that addicts feel things more intensely than other people;

it's just that we *prioritize* those feelings so much. We love dopamine and feel entitled to it. If we don't get it, we can often overanalyze, spending way too much time trying to figure out what's wrong when nothing actually is.

It's therefore crucial, in my opinion, that we start the days off right. As people in recovery circles will say, addiction can be doing push-ups when we're asleep—meaning we may not wake up hungover or drunk or high, but that same "stinking thinking" that got us to over-imbibe can be ruling our thinking.

Mornings are now something I look forward to—and I believe every person in recovery can as well. I truly believe that if people in recovery can have miracle mornings, they can all have miraculous lives.

A NOTE FROM JOE POLISH

"Recovery didn't open up the gates of heaven to let me in. But it did open up the gates of hell to let me out"

—ANONYMOUS

If there's anything I believe about addiction, it's that "the issues are in the tissues." In other words, like my dear friend Dr. Gabor Mate says, I believe addiction is a response to trauma. As I see it, addiction is a solution. The problem is that it's an ineffective solution.

The Four Elements of Recovery

In my experience, addiction can be alleviated by improving four main areas, starting first thing in the morning. These areas are community, health, environment and working through the issues that caused you to develop your addiction.

When we engage in addictive behavior, we're trying to fill a void. As Bill Wilson, one of the co-founders of Alcoholics Anonymous, said, "We're trying to drink God out of a bottle." But you don't have to be religious to want to connect. That's why I believe that the opposite of addiction isn't sobriety so much as it is connection.

The Issues I've Worked Through

While, of course, we all have struggles, my childhood was challenging: my mother passed away when I was four years old. A former nun who wrote some of the first books to teach kids to read using the phonetic method, my mother was the love of my father's life. He never got over her death and never remarried.

I have one brother who is four years older than me. We never had much of a sense of a stable home life. I was shy and introverted, and my dad dealt with his feelings by constantly moving us. But that wasn't as traumatic for me as the fact that I was sexually molested and raped between the ages of eight and ten by someone I knew and was paid money not to say anything. This was a very confusing thing for me to experience or to make sense of at that age.

As a result, I internalized a great deal of shame and believed the world wasn't safe. I had absolutely no self-esteem. And the only way I could cope with how terrible I felt was to do drugs. I kept a bong in my locker in high school and quickly moved on to taking speed and then snorting cocaine and crystal meth. By the time I was eighteen, I was smoking cocaine, and at my worst state I weighed 105 pounds.

I Quit Drugs but Addiction Played Whack-a-Mole

I'm convinced that the only reason I was able to quit drugs is because I changed my environment. For me, that meant moving in with my dad in a trailer in Las Cruces, New Mexico. But you don't need to move in order to change your environment; an environmental change can mean anything from keeping flowers in a vase next to your bed to replacing shades with curtains to getting a pet to any number of other things.

For me, once I was in a new environment and away from all the people I used drugs with, I enrolled in college and got a job selling gym memberships. I was able to build up wonderful career skills from there—a process I describe in more detail later in this book.

But, as some of you may have also experienced, getting what you think is important doesn't heal core issues. Instead of looking at my trauma and trying to figure out how it was still impacting me, I transferred my addiction to work and sex. If I'd had the knowledge I do now and been able to start my days off on the right foot, I would have been able to face the fact that I didn't know how to have intimate relationships that involved sexuality. I woke up in emotional pain, ignored it, and stayed in that pain all day. One of the few things that made the pain go away was to hire escorts and sleep with lots of women, so that's what I did; I pursued toxic relationships.

It took years of internal work for me to be able to talk about that, and I know I wouldn't have been able to if I hadn't developed a solid community and worked on my health, brain, and environment.

I've learned over the years that there's a big difference between secrecy and privacy and that you're "only as sick as your secrets," as the AA saying goes. Addicts seek chaos, and that chaos can come in the form of gambling, food, sex, performance, achievement, screens, stimulation, drugs, alcohol, caffeine, sugar, porn and many other avenues. If you've conquered your addiction to substances but are still struggling with other addictions, let me assure you that there is a solution—and it starts in the morning.

How I Hope to Be Part of Your Morning Routine

I cannot stress enough the importance of putting yourself in the right frame of mind as quickly as you can. If you wake up on the proverbial wrong side of the bed, you run the risk of staying there for the rest of the day, week, month and life. These days, I can honestly say that my mornings are miraculous and so is my life, especially when I think about where I came from.

That's why it's become my mission to help anyone who is suffering from addiction and it's why I'm now focusing my attention on two passion projects. One is Genius Recovery, a platform designed to help change the global conversation about addiction to one of treating addicts with compassion instead of judgment, along with finding and sharing the best forms of effective treatment. Because I do not believe you can punish the pain out of people. The other focus is Artists for Addicts, a project designed around using art as a force for good, which pays tribute to the many artists, writers, musicians, painters, sculptors, and actors we've lost to addiction. If you're struggling with addiction, I hope you'll read the letter I send to addicts when they contact me, which I've posted on the Genius Recovery home page (GeniusRecovery.com). And I hope you'll make Genius Recovery and Artists for Addicts (ArtistsforAddicts.com) places you stop by— every morning if you want to. My goal is that it will help make your mornings, and your life, as miraculous as it can be.

—Joe Polish

A NOTE FROM HAL

Welcome to *The Miracle Morning*. I think it's safe for us to say that there is at least one thing we have in common (probably a lot more than just *one*, but at least one that we know for sure): *We want to improve our lives and ourselves.* This is not to suggest that there is anything necessarily "wrong" with us or our lives, but as human beings we were born with the innate desire and drive to continuously grow and improve. I believe it's within all of us. Yet, we all wake up each day, and, for most of us, life pretty much stays the same.

Whatever your life is like right now—whether you are currently experiencing extraordinary levels of success, enduring the most challenging time of your life, or somewhere in between, I can say with absolute certainty that *The Miracle Morning* is the most practical, results-oriented, and effective method I have ever encountered for improving any—or quite literally **every**—area of your life, and doing so faster than you may even believe is possible.

For achievers and top performers, *The Miracle Morning* can be an absolute game-changer, allowing you to attain that elusive *next level* and take your personal and professional success far beyond what you've achieved up until this point. While this can include increasing your income or growing your business, sales, and revenue, it's often more about discovering new ways to experience deeper levels of fulfillment and success in aspects of your life that you may have neglected. This can mean making significant improvements with your **health**, **happiness**, **relationships**, **finances**, **spirituality**, or any other areas that are at the top of your list.

For those who are in the midst of adversity and enduring times of struggle—be it mental, emotional, physical, financial, relational, or other—*The Miracle Morning* has proven time and time again to be the one thing that can empower anyone to overcome seemingly insurmountable challenges, make major breakthroughs, and turn their circumstances around, often in a very short period of time.

Whether you want to make significant improvements in just a few key areas or you are ready for a major overhaul that will radically transform your entire life—so your current circumstances will soon become only a memory of what was—you've picked up the right book. You are about to begin a miraculous journey, using a simple step-by-step process that is guaranteed to transform any area of your life…all before 8:00 a.m.

I know, I know—these are some big promises to make. But *The Miracle Morning* is already generating measurable results for hundreds of thousands of people around the world, and it can absolutely be the one thing that takes you to where you want to be. My co-authors and I have done everything in our power to ensure that this book will truly be a life-changing investment of your time, energy, and attention. Thank you for allowing us to be a part of your life. Our miraculous journey together is about to begin.

With love & gratitude ~ Hal

SECTION I:

THE MIRACLE MORNING
+
LIFE S.A.V.E.R.S

— 1 —

WHY MORNINGS MATTER
(MORE THAN YOU THINK)

*"You've got to wake up every morning with determination
if you're going to go to bed with satisfaction."*

–GEORGE LORIMER,
American journalist and author

*"Damn right I live the life I live,
'cause I went from negative to positive."*

—BIGGIE SMALLS,
a.k.a. The Notorious B.I.G,

How you start each morning sets your mindset—and the context—for the rest of your day. Start every day with a purposeful, disciplined, growth-infused, and goal-oriented morning, and you're virtually guaranteed to crush your day. Or, at the very least, start off strong.

If you start off your day feeling overwhelmed, congratulations—you're a person in recovery from addiction. You're also suffering from what we like to call humanism. Our brains are programmed to look for dangers, which means we're all slightly slanted toward negativity (with the exception of those people you meet who somehow seem to have natural Prozac running through their veins). If you don't set an alarm clock (or, hello, in this day and age, an alarm in your phone), then you perhaps open your eyes and immediately hear the "committee" (those voices in your head that seem so loud it's like they were doing push-ups when you were asleep) yammering about all the things they haven't done yet or will never do. Recovery doesn't always guarantee sanity, or even healthy thinking. As George Carlin famously said, "Just because you got the monkey off your back doesn't mean the circus has left town."

What if you could have that hour of peace and quiet you've been dreaming about? That clean, uncluttered mental space where you could regain your sense of elegance and dignity, where you're in total control and can proceed in an orderly, self-nurturing fashion? But you know you can't—or maybe you can, but not today. Maybe when you're twenty years sober. Or when you've accomplished everything you need to in order to make up for all the time you wasted drinking and using.

It's no wonder most addicts start their days with procrastination, letting whatever happens to befall them set the agenda and sending a message to their subconscious that says they don't have enough energy or even the will to get out of bed. They think today will be another free-for-all where their personal goals go out the window in the usual scramble to meet others' needs (or to indulge in *Game of Throne* marathons enhanced by regular consumption of Ben and Jerry's).

Add to this the fact that most people believe they aren't early risers, and the pattern of procrastination shows up early in life.

But what if you could change it?

What if you could consider the alarm clock beeping or your eyes popping open in the morning to be life's first gift? It's the gift of time that you can dedicate to becoming the person you need to be to achieve all your goals and dreams—while the rest of the world is still asleep.

You might be thinking, *All of this sounds great, Joe and Anna. But. I. Am. Not. A. Morning. Person.*

We understand. We really do! You're not saying anything we haven't told ourselves a thousand times before. And believe us, we tried—and failed—many times to take control of our mornings. But that was before we discovered *The Miracle Morning.*

Stay with us here. In addition to wanting to be free from the addiction, we bet you also want to stop worrying about having more month than money, quit missing your goals, and release the occasionally crippling emotions that can accompany those challenges. Let's say that someone said to you, "Hey, want to stop doing those things that get in the way of being an effective and happy person because they affect your self-esteem and prevent you from feeling good about yourself and your life?" You might first note that this was an extremely long sentence. You would probably then answer, "Why yes. Yes, I would."

We're firm believers in the advice given at the start of every airplane flight: *put your oxygen mask on first, and then help your child.* You won't be able to help anyone if you pass out due to lack of oxygen.

Many addicts don't see this simple truth. They think that success means putting their own needs last, and then they have so much to do that they never get to those needs. Over time, they end up exhausted, depressed, resentful, and overwhelmed. There's a word for this: codependent. But even those of us who don't wrestle with codependency can put other people's needs before our own.

If this rings true for you, know this:

Mornings are the key to all of it.

More important than even the *time* that you start your day is the *mindset* with which you start your day.

Although there's a chance you're reading this book after years of being in recovery, you may also be in the early stages of your journey, which means that feeling overwhelmed is the norm. You're supposed to be looking for answers right now (and always). If that's the case, then learning to practice your Miracle Morning before anything else is important to make sure you get your time, uninterrupted. The good news is that it's worth it, and if you're someone who spent a lot of time seeking out quick and easy fixes, we bet you'll be shocked by how fun and rewarding it can be.

But, before we get into exactly *how* you can master your mornings, let us make the case for *why*. Because, believe us, once you've uncovered the truth about mornings, you'll lament the fact that you spent so many nursing a hangover (or sleeping).

Why Mornings Matter So Much

The more you explore the power of early rising and morning rituals, the more proof mounts that the early bird gets *a lot* more than the worm. Here are just a few of the key advantages you're about to learn for yourself:

- **You'll be more proactive and productive.** Christoph Randler is a professor of biology at the University of Education in Heidelberg, Germany. In the July 2010 issue of *Harvard Business Review*, Randler found that "people whose performance peaks in the morning are better positioned for career success, because they're more proactive than people who are at their best in the evening." According to *New York Times* best-selling author and world-renowned entrepreneur Robin Sharma, "If you study many of the most productive people in the world, they all had one thing in common—they were early risers."

- **You'll anticipate problems and head them off at the pass.** Randler went on to conclude that morning people hold all of the important cards. They are "better able to anticipate and minimize problems, are proactive, have greater professional success and ultimately make higher wages." He noted morning people are able to anticipate problems and handle them with grace and ease. If you think about it, this could be the key to decreasing the level of stress that comes with facing reality when you don't have any chemicals shrouding your feelings.

- **You'll plan like a pro.** Planning is very important when it comes to exceptional recovery. It's been said that *when we fail to plan, we are indirectly planning to fail*. Morning folks have the time to organize, anticipate, and prepare for their day. Our sleepy counterparts are reactive, leaving a lot to chance. Aren't you more stressed when you sleep through your alarm? Getting up with the sun (or before) lets you jump-start your day. While everyone else is running around trying (and failing) to get their day under control, you'll be more calm, cool, and collected.

- **You'll have more energy.** One component of your new Miracle Mornings will be morning exercise, which often is something neglected by busy people in recovery. Yet, in as little as a few minutes, exercise sets a positive tone for the day. Increased blood to the brain will help you think more clearly and focus on what's most important. Fresh oxygen will permeate every cell in your body and increase your energy, which is why people in recovery who exercise are in a better mood and in better shape, get better sleep, and become more productive.

- **You'll gain early bird attitude advantages.** Recently, researchers at the University of Barcelona in Spain compared morning people (those early birds who like to get up at dawn) with evening people (those night owls who prefer to stay up late and sleep in). Among the differences, they found that morning people tend to be more persistent and resistant to fatigue, frustration, and difficulties. That translates into lower levels of anxiety, rates of depression, and—hello!—likelihood of substance abuse. A better attitude has helped us create a more powerful mindset, which has made us better friends, employers and people—and has helped us have more fruitful and satisfying lives.

The evidence is in, and the experts have had their say. *Mornings contain the secret to an extraordinarily successful life.*

Mornings? Really?

We admit it. To go from *I'm not a morning person* to *I really want to become a morning person* to *I'm up early every morning, and it feels amazing!* is a process. But after some trial and error, you will discover how to outfox, preempt and foil your inner late sleeper so you can make early rising a habit. Okay, sounds great in theory, but you might be shaking your head and telling yourself, "There's no way. I'm already cramming 27 hours of stuff into 24 hours. How on earth could I get up an hour earlier than I already do?"

We ask: "How can you not?"

The key thing to understand is that the Miracle Morning isn't about denying yourself an hour of sleep so you can have an even longer, harder day. It's not even about waking up earlier. It's about waking up *better*.

Thousands of people around the planet are already living their own Miracle Mornings. Many of them were night owls. But they're making it work. In fact, they're *thriving*. And it's not because they simply added an hour to their day. It's because they added *the right* hour. And so can you.

Still skeptical? Then let us tell you this: *The hardest part about getting up an hour earlier is the first five minutes.* That's the crucial time when, tucked into your warm bed, you make the decision to start your day or hit the snooze button *just one more time*. It's the moment of truth, and the decision you make right then will change your day, your success, and your life.

And that's why the first five minutes is the starting point for *The Miracle Morning for Addiction and Recovery*. It's time for you to win every morning! When we win our mornings, we win the day.

In the next two chapters, we'll make waking up early easier and more exciting than it's ever been in your life (even if you've *never* considered yourself to be a morning person) and show you how to maximize those newfound morning minutes with the Life S.A.V.E.R.S.—the six most powerful, proven personal development practices known to man.

Chapters four, five, and six will reveal not-so-obvious recovery principles related to accelerating your personal growth, why you need to structure your life to gain endless amounts of energy, and how to optimize your ability to stay focused on your goals and what matters most.

Finally, chapters seven, eight, nine, and ten cover the critical skills you'll want to master to live the healthiest, happiest and most fruitful life in recovery. There's even a bonus chapter from Hal tacked on at the end.

We have a lot of ground to cover in this book, so let's jump right in.

RECOVERY WARRIOR MIRACLE MORNING ROUTINE

MACKENZIE PHILLIPS

FACEBOOK.COM/MACKENZIE-PHILLIPS -296797666085

TWITTER/INSTAGRAM: @MACKPHILLIPS

Mackenzie Phillips is an American actress and author best known for her roles in *American Graffiti* and as rebellious teenager Julie Mora Cooper Horvath on the sitcom *One Day at a Time.*

Having struggled with drug and alcohol abuse for over a decade, Phillips has utilized her platform as a public figure to help educate people about addiction and to combat social stigmas. Her 2009 memoir, *High on Arrival,* detailed her battle with substance abuse and family trauma throughout her life and her subsequent journey to mental and physical wellness.

Turning her life around to find that her passion is helping others to do the same, Phillips became a primary substance use counselor in 2013 and began working in the treatment field. Phillips currently works as a substance use disorder counselor at Breathe Life Healing Centers in West Hollywood, CA.

Phillips is the author of *Hopeful Healing: Essays on Managing Recovery* and *Surviving Addiction* (Beyond Words/Atria, 02/07/2017) and is one of the most visible and outspoken advocates for addiction awareness and education in America.

Mackenzie's morning routine:

- My alarm is set for 6:00 a.m....and 6:05 a.m....and finally 6:15 a.m....

- I welcome the morning with kisses to my pups, snuggles with Mrs. Cat, and a genuine and loving "thank you" to God, the Universe, all who went before me, and my loving friends and family.

- Then, it's nuts and bolts, which I find meditative: make the coffee, feed the creatures, check the email, wash the face, apply the make-up, write the loving morning note to the kid (30-year-old Shane).

- My routine has a rhythm all its own, like a percussive motion that motivates and inspires me to do the deal. Can you feel the beat? I can, and it's a good one.

IT ONLY TAKES FIVE MINUTES TO BECOME A MORNING PERSON

"If you really think about it, hitting the snooze button in the morning doesn't even make sense. It's like saying, "I hate getting up in the morning, so I do it over, and over, and over again."
—DEMETRI MARTIN, Comedian

"Good morning. On this day we become legendary."
—KANYE WEST

If you've been living your life believing, as so many of us are taught, that the most important factor in our day is what happens to us throughout it, we've got news for you: it's actually how you start your day that's the most important factor in determining how we live our lives. When we wake up with the excitement we might have felt back when we were calling the dealer, firing up the porn or pouring the vino and instead create a purposeful, powerful, productive morning, we set ourselves up to win the day.

Yet, most people start their day with resistance and procrastination, hitting the snooze button and waiting until the last possible moment to pry themselves out from beneath their cozy covers. We get it—covers can be damn cozy! But while it may not be obvious, this seemingly innocent act may actually be sending a detrimental message to our subconscious, programming our psyche with the unconscious belief that we don't have the self-discipline to get out of bed in the morning, let alone do what's necessary to achieve everything else we want for our lives. The committee that chatters away in your head then has a chance to make up a whole crazy story about the other things you may lack—all while you're trying to get back to that dream you were having about going horseback riding with Woody Harrelson (hey, we don't judge).

Could it be that how we wake up in the morning is impacting who we're becoming, and thus impacting every area of our lives?

When the alarm starts beeping in the morning, consider it life's first *gift*, *challenge*, and *opportunity* to us—all three at the same time—each day. It's the gift of another day, the challenge of making the disciplined decision to get out of bed, and the opportunity to invest time into our personal development so each of us can become the person we need to be to create the life we truly want. And we get to do all of this while the rest of the world continues to sleep. And let's be honest: from party favors when we were little through the extra freebie the drug dealer would hand over if you were a really good customer, who doesn't love a gift?

However, if it weren't for this strategy that you're about to learn, we'd still be snoozing through the alarm clock every morning and clinging to our old limiting belief that we were *not morning people.*

The good news is that it is possible to love waking up—and do it easily, each day—even if you've *never* been a morning person.

We know you might not believe it. Right now, you might think *that might be true for early birds but trust me, I've tried. I'm just not a morning person.*

But it is true. We know because we've been there. Anna used to take sleep medication before she went to bed and in the middle of the night whenever she woke up. She used to sleep until the last possible moment, when she absolutely had to wake up. She dreaded mornings. She hated waking up.

And now we both love it.

How did we do it? When people ask us how we transformed ourselves into morning people—and transformed our lives in the process—we tell them we did it in five simple steps, one at a time. We know it may seem downright impossible. But take it from former snooze-aholics: you can do this. And you can do it the same way we did.

That's the critical message about waking up—it's possible to change. Morning people aren't born—they're self-made. If you're an alcoholic or addict who quit drinking, gambling, acting out sexually or doing drugs, this is cake! You can do it, and it doesn't require the willpower of an Olympic marathoner. We contend that when early rising becomes not only something you do, but *who you are,* you will truly love mornings. Waking up will become for you like it is for us—effortless.

Not convinced? Suspend your disbelief a little and let us introduce you to the five-step process that changed our lives. Five simple, snooze-proof keys that made waking up in the morning—even early in the morning—easier than ever before. Without this strategy, we would still be sleeping (or snoozing) through the alarm(s) each morning. Worse, we would still be clinging to the limiting belief that we are not morning people.

And we would have missed a whole world of opportunity.

The Challenge with Waking Up

Waking up earlier is a bit like running: you think you're not a runner—maybe you even *hate* running—until you lace up a pair of running shoes and reluctantly head out the front door at a pace that suggests you might be about to go for a run. With a commitment to overcome your seemingly insurmountable hatred for running, you put one foot in front of the other. Do this for a few weeks and one day it hits you: *I've become a runner.*

Similarly, if you've resisted waking up in the morning and chose to hit the *procrastination*—er, *snooze*—button, then of course you're not *yet* a morning person. But if you follow the simple step-by-step process that you're about to discover, you'll wake up in a few weeks (maybe even a few days) and it will hit you: *OMG, I can't believe it… I've become a morning person!*

However, right now, you might be feeling motivated, excited, optimistic. But what happens tomorrow morning when that alarm goes off? How motivated will you be when you're yanked out of a deep sleep in a warm bed by a screaming alarm clock in a cold house?

We all know where motivation will be right then. It will be flushed down the toilet and replaced by rationalization. And rationalization is a crafty master—in seconds, we can convince ourselves that we just need a few extra minutes…

…and the next thing we know, we're scrambling around the house late for work, late for life. Again.

It's a tricky problem. The time when we need our motivation the most—those first few moments of the day—is precisely when we seem to have the least of it.

The solution, then, is to boost that morning motivation and mount a surprise attack on rationalization. That's what these five steps do for you. Each step in the process is designed to increase what Hal calls your Wake-Up Motivation Level (WUML).

First thing in the morning, you might have a low WUML, meaning you want nothing more than to go back to sleep when your alarm goes off. That's normal. But by using this simple five-step process (that takes about five minutes), you can generate a high WUML, where you're ready to jump up and embrace the day.

The Five-Step Snooze-Proof Wake-Up Strategy

Minute One: Think About the Intentions You Set *Before* Bedtime

The first key to waking up is to understand this: *your first thought in the morning is usually the same as your last thought before you went to sleep.* We bet, for example, that you've had nights where you could hardly fall asleep because you were so excited about waking up the next morning. Whether it was when you were a kid on Christmas morning or the day you were leaving for a big vacation, as soon as the alarm clock sounded, you opened your eyes ready to jump out of bed and embrace the day. Why? It's because the last thought you had about the coming morning—before you fell asleep—was positive.

On the other hand, if your last thought before bed was something like: *Oh gosh, I can't believe I have to get up in six hours—I'm going to be exhausted in the morning!* then your first thought when the alarm clock goes off is likely to be something like, *Oh gosh, it's already been six hours? Nooo…I'm too tired to wake up!* Consider that it is a self-fulfilling prophecy, and you create your own reality.

The first step, then, is to consciously decide—every night, before bed—to actively and mindfully create a positive expectation for the next morning. Visualize it, and affirm it to yourself.

For help on this and to get the precise words to say before bed to create your powerful morning intentions, download *The Miracle Morning Bedtime Affirmations* free at www.TMMBook.com .

Minute Two: Get Out of Bed to Turn Your Alarm Off

If you haven't done so already, be sure to move your alarm clock or phone as far from your bed as possible. This will make it inevitable that you have to actually get out of bed and engage your body in movement to start each day. Motion creates energy, so getting out of bed and walking across the room naturally helps you to wake up.

Most people keep their alarm next to their bed, within reach. Think about it: if you keep your alarm within reach, then you're still in a partial sleep state after the alarm goes off, and your wake-up motivation level (a.k.a. your WUML) is at its lowest point, which makes it much more difficult to summon the discipline to get out of bed. In fact, you may turn off the alarm without even realizing it! On more than a few occasions, we've all convinced ourselves that our alarm was merely part of the dream we were having. (You're not alone on that one, trust us.)

By forcing yourself to get out of bed to turn off the alarm, you are setting yourself up for early rising success by instantly increasing your WUML.

However, on a scale of one to ten, your WUML may still be hovering around a five, and you'll likely be feeling sleepier than not, so the temptation to turn around and crawl back into bed will still be present. To raise that WUML just a little further, try …

Minute Three: Brush Your Teeth

As soon as you've gotten out of bed and turned off your alarm, go directly to the bathroom sink to brush your teeth. We know what you may be thinking: *Really? You're telling me that I need to brush my teeth?* Yes. The point is that you're doing mindless activities for the first few minutes and simply giving your body time to wake up.

After brushing your teeth, splash some warm (or cold) water on your face. This simple activity will allow for the passing of more time to increase your WUML even further.

Now that your mouth is minty fresh, it's time to …

Minute Four: Drink a Full Glass of Water

It's crucial that you hydrate yourself first thing every morning. After six to eight hours without water, you'll be mildly dehydrated, which causes fatigue. Often, when people feel tired—at any time of the day—what they really need is more water, not more sleep.

Start by getting a glass or bottle of water (or you can do what we do and fill it up the night before so it's already there for you in the morning) and drink it as fast as is comfortable for you. The objective is to replace the water you were deprived of during the hours you slept. (And hey, the side benefits of morning hydration are better, younger-looking skin and maintaining a healthy weight. Not bad for a few ounces of water!)

That glass of water should raise your WUML another notch, which will get you to …

Minute Five: Get Dressed in Your Workout Clothes (or Jump in the Shower)

The fifth step has two options. *Option one* is to get dressed in your exercise clothing so you're ready to leave your bedroom and immediately engage in your Miracle Morning. You can lay out your clothes before you go to bed or even sleep in your workout clothes. (Yes, really.) And for addicts in recovery, the "night before" prep is especially important to help you go straight into your practice. If you have kids, you can make this a part of their bedtime ritual so they build the habit too.

Option two is to jump in the shower, which is a great way to finish off taking your WUML to the point where staying awake is much easier. However, Joe usually opts to change into exercise clothes since he'll need a shower after working out, and he believes there is something to be said about *earning* your morning shower! But a lot of people prefer the morning shower because it helps them wake up and gives them a fresh start to the day. The choice is completely yours.

Regardless of which option you choose, by the time you've executed these five simple steps, your WUML should be high enough that it requires very little discipline to stay awake for your Miracle Morning.

If you were to try to make that commitment the moment your alarm clock first went off—while you were at a WUML of nearly zero—it would be a much more difficult decision to make. The five steps let you build momentum so that, within just a few minutes, you're ready to go instead of feeling groggy.

Miracle Morning Bonus Wake-Up Tips

Although this strategy has worked for thousands of people, these five steps are not the only way to make waking up in the morning easier. Here are a few others we've heard from fellow Miracle Morning practitioners:

- The Miracle Morning Bedtime Affirmations: If you haven't done this yet, take a moment now to go to www.TMMbook.

com and download the re-energizing, intention-setting Bedtime Affirmations for free. Nothing is more effective for ensuring that you will wake up eager to start your day than programming your mind to achieve exactly what you want.

- Set a timer for your bedroom lights: One member of The Miracle Morning Community shared that he sets his bedroom lights on a timer (you can buy an appliance timer online or at your local hardware store). As his alarm goes off, the lights come on in the room. What a great idea! It's a lot easier to fall back asleep when it's dark—having the lights on tells your mind and body that it's time to wake up. (Whether you use a timer or not, be sure to turn your light on right after you turn your alarm off.)

- Set a timer for your bedroom heater: Another member of *The Miracle Morning Community* says that in the winter, she keeps a bedroom heater on an appliance timer set to turn on fifteen minutes before she wakes up. She keeps her bedroom cold at night but warm for waking up so she won't be tempted to crawl back under her covers.

Feel free to add to or customize the Five-Step Snooze-Proof Wake-Up Strategy, and if you have any tips that you're open to sharing, we'd love to hear them. Please post them in The Miracle Morning Community at www.MyTMMCommunity.com.

Waking up consistently and easily is all about having an effective, predetermined, step-by-step strategy to increase your WUML in the morning. Don't wait to try this! Start tonight by reading The Miracle Morning Bedtime Affirmations to set a powerful intention for waking up tomorrow morning, moving your alarm clock across the room, setting a glass of water on your nightstand, and committing to the other two steps for the morning.

Taking Immediate Action

There's no need to wait to get started implementing the power of early rising. As Tony Robbins has said, "When is NOW a good time for you to do that?" Now, indeed, would be perfect! In fact, the sooner you start, the sooner you'll begin to see results, including increased energy, a better attitude, and, of course, a happier home life.

Step One: Set your alarm for thirty to sixty minutes earlier than you usually wake up, for the next thirty days. That's it; just thirty to sixty minutes for thirty days, starting now. And be sure to write into your schedule to do your first Miracle Morning *tomorrow morning.* That's right, don't using *waiting until you finish the book* as an excuse to procrastinate on getting started!

If you're feeling resistant at all, maybe because you've tried to make changes in the past but haven't followed through, here's a suggestion: turn now to "Chapter 11: The Miracle Morning 30-Day Transformation Challenge" and read ahead. This will not only give you the mindset and strategy to overcome any resistance you may have to getting started but also the most effective process for implementing a new habit and sticking with it. Think of it as beginning with the end in mind.

From this day forward, starting with the next thirty days, keep your alarm set for thirty to sixty minutes earlier than you (or your children) typically wake up so that you can start waking up when you *want* to, instead of when you *have* to. It's time to start launching each day with a Miracle Morning so that you can become the person you need to be to take yourself, your children, and your family to extraordinary levels.

What will you do with that hour? You're going to find out in the next chapter, but for now, simply continue reading this book during your Miracle Morning until you learn the whole routine.

Step Two: Join The Miracle Morning Community at www.MyTMMCommunity.com to connect with and get support from more than 100,000 like-minded early risers, many of whom have been generating extraordinary results with the Miracle Morning for years.

Step Three: Find a Miracle Morning accountability partner. Enroll someone—your spouse, a friend, family member, coworker, or someone you meet in The Miracle Morning Community—to join you on this adventure so you can encourage, support, and hold each other accountable to follow through until your Miracle Morning has become a lifelong habit.

Okay, now let's get into the six most powerful, proven personal development practices known to man (or woman): The Life S.A.V.E.R.S.

RECOVERY WARRIOR MORNING ROUTINE

COURTNEY FRIEL
FACEBOOK.COM/COURTNEYFRIEL
TWITTER/INSTAGRAM: @COURTNEYFRIEL

Courtney is a news anchor and reporter at KTLA in Los Angeles. Before that, she spent six years as a correspondent at Fox News channel in NYC. She worked her way up through local news and has also had hosting gigs at E! and on the World Poker Tour. Her biggest accomplishment, however, is being a mom to her 7-year-old son and 6-year-old daughter.

Courtney's morning routine:

- I always wake up and see the sign next to my bed that says, "Today is a good day for a good day." It sets the tone for my day and serves as a reminder to immediately thank God for all of my blessings and another day alive.

- On days I have the kids, I take them to school, then come back and go out on my balcony, which I made all Zen. I drink my cup of coffee in my comfy chair and meditate for twenty minutes. Then I either work out on my elliptical, with my trainer, or in a yoga class.

- On days that I report at 8 a.m., I always say to my photographers a mantra I created. Tony Robbins says if you ask your brain questions, it will look for the answers throughout the day. This is mine: "Who are we going to meet today, what are we going to learn today, who are we going to help today, how much fun will we have today, and how low stress of a day are we going to have?"

— 3 —
THE LIFE S.A.V.E.R.S.

Six Practices Guaranteed to Save You from a Life of Unfulfilled Potential

What Hal has done with his acronym S.A.V.E.R.S. is take the best practices—developed over centuries of human consciousness development—and condensed the "best of the best" into a daily morning ritual. A ritual that is now part of my day.

*Many people do one of the S.A.V.E.R.S. daily. For example, many people do the **E**, they exercise every morning. Others do **S** for silence or meditation, or **S** for scribing or journaling. But until Hal packaged S.A.V.E.R.S., no one was doing all six ancient "best practices" every morning. The Miracle Morning is perfect for very busy, successful people. Going through S.A.V.E.R.S. every morning is like pumping rocket fuel into my body, mind, and spirit … before I start my day, every day.*

—ROBERT KIYOSAKI, Best-Selling author of *Rich Dad Poor Dad*

Most people live their lives on the wrong side of a significant gap that separates who we are from who we can become, which holds us back from creating the life we truly want. Often frustrated with ourselves and our lack of consistent motivation, effort and results in one or more areas of life, we spend too much time *thinking* about the actions we should be taking to create the results that we want, but then we don't take those actions. More often than not, we know what we need to do…we just don't consistently *do* what we know.

Do you ever feel like that? Like the life and recovery that you want, and the person you know you need to be to create both, are just beyond your grasp? When you see others in recovery who are excelling in an area, or playing at a level that you're not, does it ever seem like they've got it all figured out? Like they must know something that you don't know, because if you knew it, then you'd be excelling too?

When Hal experienced the second of his two rock bottoms (the first was when he died for six minutes in a car crash, and the second was when his business failed due to the financial collapse of 2008), he felt lost and depressed. Applying what he already knew wasn't working. Nothing he tried was improving his situation. So, he began his own quest for the fastest, most effective strategy to take his success to the next level. He went in search of the best personal development practices that were being practiced by the world's most successful people.

After discovering and assembling a list of six of the most timeless, effective, and proven personal development practices, he first attempted to determine which one or two would accelerate his success the fastest. However, his breakthrough occurred when he asked himself, *what would happen if I did ALL of these?*

So, he did. Within just two months of implementing all six practices nearly every single day, Hal experienced what you might call "miraculous" results. He was able to more than double his income, and he went from someone who had never run more than a mile to training to run a 52-mile ultramarathon—ironic because he *wasn't* a runner and actually despised running. He thought, *What better way to take my physical, mental, emotional, and spiritual capacities to another level?*

Whether you're already very successful, like multi-millionaire entrepreneur Robert Kiyosaki (who practices the Miracle Morning and the S.A.V.E.R.S. almost every day), or if you've ever felt like the life you want to live, and the person you know you can be, are just beyond your grasp, the Life S.A.V.E.R.S. are virtually guaranteed to save you from missing out on the extraordinary life you truly want.

Why the S.A.V.E.R.S. Work

The S.A.V.E.R.S. are simple but profoundly effective daily morning practices that enable you to achieve more so that you can fulfill your potential. They also give you space to gain heightened levels of clarity so you can plan and live your life on your terms. They're designed to start your day by putting you in a peak physical, mental, emotional, and spiritual state so that you continuously improve, feel great, and ALWAYS perform at your best.

We know. You don't have time. Before starting the Miracle Morning, Anna thought she had a solid morning routine because she woke up, read a spiritual newsletter she subscribed to, and then got back into bed to meditate. What she didn't take into account, when she was starting her day on this spiritual quest, was that the first thing she was actually doing was checking her phone (because that's where she received her email). No matter how diligently she tried to ignore the work emails that had filtered in overnight and only focus on the daily newsletter to set her in the right frame of mind to begin her meditation practice, she couldn't help but scan the others. Those emails are what she had in her head during the twenty minutes she attempted to focus on the mantra her Vedic Meditation teacher had given her. Afterwards, she'd do a quick prayer and go right to the computer to answer whatever emails she'd ingested twenty-one minutes earlier, and the time she'd devoted to "waking up right" had flitted away, along with whatever helpful information was in her spiritual newsletter.

Joe's travel schedule is so extreme that his morning routine for a while varied between either practicing twenty minutes of meditation or starting right in on burpees (explained in much more detail later in this book).

You probably think you can hardly squeeze in what you already have to do, never mind what you want to do. But we "didn't have time" before the Miracle Morning either. And yet, here we are, with more time, more prosperity, and more peaceful lives than we've ever had before.

What you need to realize right now is that your Miracle Morning will create time for you. The Life S.A.V.E.R.S. are the vehicle to help you reconnect with your true essence and wake up with purpose instead of obligation. The practices help you build energy, see priorities more clearly, and find the most productive flow in your life.

In other words, the Life S.A.V.E.R.S. don't take time from your day but ultimately add more to it.

Each letter in S.A.V.E.R.S. represents one of the best practices of the most successful people on the planet. From A-list movie stars and world-class professional athletes to CEOs and entrepreneurs, you'd be hard pressed to find an elite performer who didn't swear by at least one of the S.A.V.E.R.S.

However, you'd be equally hard-pressed to find an elite performer who practices even half—let alone ALL of the S.A.V.E.R.S. (Although, not to toot Hal's horn, but that's changing now that Hal has introduced the world to the Miracle Morning.) That's what makes the Miracle Morning so effective; you're harnessing the game-changing benefits of not just one but all six of *the best success practices, developed over centuries of human consciousness development* and combining them all into a concise, fully customizable morning ritual.

The S.A.V.E.R.S. are:

Silence

Affirmations

Visualization

Exercise

Reading

Scribing

Leveraging these six practices is how you will accelerate your personal development by maximizing the impact of your newfound Miracle Morning ritual. They're customizable to fit you, your lifestyle, your business, and your specific goals. And you can start implementing them first thing tomorrow morning.

Let's go through each of the S.A.V.E.R.S. in detail.

S is for Silence

Silence, the first practice of the Life S.A.V.E.R.S., is a key habit for a healthy recovery. If you've been guilty of starting your day by immediately grabbing your phone or computer and diving into emails, phone calls, social media, and text messages, then this is your opportunity to learn the power of beginning each day with peaceful, purposeful *silence*.

Like we did before we discovered the Miracle Morning, most people start the day when their alarm signifies they *must* get up. And most people run from morning to night, struggling to regain control for the rest of the day. It's not a coincidence. Starting each day with a period of silence instead will immediately reduce your stress levels and help you begin the day with the kind of calm and clarity that you need to focus on what's most important.

Remember, many of the world's most successful people are daily practitioners of silence. That shows you how important it is. It's not surprising that Oprah practices stillness—or that she does nearly all the other Life S.A.V.E.R.S. too. Musician Katy Perry practices Transcendental Meditation, as do Sheryl Crow and Sir Paul McCartney. Film and television stars Jennifer Aniston, Ellen DeGeneres, Jerry Seinfeld, Howard Stern, Cameron Diaz, Clint Eastwood, and Hugh Jackman have all spoken of their daily meditation practice. Even famous billionaires Ray Dalio and Rupert Murdoch have attributed their financial success to the daily practice of stillness. You'll be in good (and quiet) company by doing the same.

If it seems like we're asking you to do nothing, let us clarify: you have many choices for your practice of silence. In no particular order, here are a few to get you started:

- Meditation
- Prayer
- Reflection
- Deep breathing
- Gratitude

Whichever you choose, be sure you don't stay in bed for your period of silence, and better still, get out of your bedroom altogether.

In an interview with *Shape* magazine, actress and singer Kristen Bell said, "Do meditative yoga for 10 minutes every morning. When you have a problem—whether it's road rage, your guy, or work—meditation allows everything to unfold the way it's supposed to."

And don't be afraid to expand your horizons. Meditation comes in many forms. As Angelina Jolie told *Stylist* magazine, "I find meditation in sitting on the floor with the kids coloring for an hour, or going on the trampoline. You do what you love, that makes you happy, and that gives you your meditation."

The Benefits of Silence

How many times do we find ourselves in stressful situations? How many times do we deal with immediate needs that take us away from our vision or plan? Stress is one of the most common side effects of the lives we live in recovery, where we often try to pack in everything we neglected when we were in active addiction. We face the ever-present distractions of other people encroaching on our schedule and the inevitable fires we must extinguish. Our triggers have the uncanny ability to push our stress buttons.

Excessive stress is terrible for your health. It triggers your fight-or-flight response, and that releases a cascade of toxic hormones that can stay in your body for days. It's fine if you experience that type of stress only occasionally.

According to PsychologyToday.com, "The stress hormone, cortisol, is public health enemy number one. Scientists have known for years that elevated cortisol levels: interfere with learning and memory, lower immune function and bone density, increase weight gain, blood pressure, cholesterol, heart disease… The list goes on and on. Chronic stress and elevated cortisol levels also increase risk for depression, mental illness, and lower life expectancy."

Silence in the form of meditation reduces stress and, as a result, improves your health. A major study run by several groups, including the National Institutes of Health, the American Medical Association, the Mayo Clinic, and scientists from both Harvard and Stanford, revealed that meditation reduces stress and high blood pressure. A recent study by Dr. Norman Rosenthal, a world-renowned psychiatrist who works with the David Lynch Foundation, even found that people who practice meditation are 30 percent less likely to die from heart disease.

Another study from Harvard found that just eight weeks of meditation could lead to "increased gray-matter density in the hippocampus, known to be important for learning and memory, and in structures associated with self-awareness, compassion, and introspection."

Meditation helps you to slow down and focus on you, even if it's for just a short time. Moms, start your meditation practice now and say goodbye to "mommy brain."

"I started meditating because I felt like I needed to stop my life from running me," singer Sheryl Crow has said. "So, meditation for me helped slow my day down." She continues to devote twenty minutes in the morning and twenty minutes at night to meditation.

Says Recovery 2.0 founder Tommy Rosen (whose morning routine we document later in the book), "From a recovery perspective, I can assert that meditation helped me transform from a stressed-out sober person to a human being on a path of discovery, and that is saying quite a lot. At first, it's decidedly un-blissful. If you run from the boogeyman your whole life and then you turn to face him, of course it's going to be uncomfortable at first. Then, after some practice, you realize there is no boogeyman, and then it really does become quite blissful, like having some time out of time. Imagine not needing or wanting anything; a moment free from any craving at all."

Being silent opens a space for you to secure your own oxygen mask before assisting others. The benefits are extraordinary and can bring you much-needed clarity and peace of mind. Practicing silence, in other words, can help you reduce your stress, improve cognitive performance, and become confident at the same time.

Guided Meditations and Meditation Apps

Meditation is like anything else—if you've never done it before, then it can be difficult or feel awkward at first. If you are a first-time meditator, we recommend starting with a guided meditation.

Here are a few of our favorite meditation apps that are available for both iPhone/iPad and Android devices:

- Headspace
- Calm
- Omvana
- Simply Being
- Insight Timer
- 10% Happier

Of course, there are subtle and significant differences among these meditation apps, one of which is the voice of the person speaking.

If you don't have a device that allows you to download apps, simply go to YouTube or Google and search for the keywords "guided meditation." You can also search by duration (i.e. "five-minute guided meditation") or topic (i.e. "guided meditation for increased confidence").

Miracle Morning (Individual) Meditation

When you're ready to try meditating on your own, here is a simple, step-by-step meditation you can use during your Miracle Morning, even if you've never done this before.

Before beginning, it's important to prepare yourself and set expectations. This is a time for you to quiet your mind and let go of the compulsive need to constantly be thinking about something— reliving the past or worrying about the future, but never living fully in the present. This is the time to let go of your stresses, take a break from worrying about your problems, and be here in this moment. It is a time to access the essence of who you truly are—to go deeper than what you have, what you do, or the labels you've accepted as who you are. If this sounds foreign to you, or too New Age-y, that's okay. Trust us, we've felt the same way. It's probably because you've never tried it before. But thankfully, you're about to.

- Find a quiet, comfortable place to sit. You can sit on the couch, on a chair, on the floor, or on a pillow for added comfort.

- Sit upright, cross-legged. You can close your eyes, or you can look down at a point on the ground about two feet in front of you.

- Begin by focusing on your breath, taking slow, deep breaths. Breathe in through the nose and out through the mouth. The most effective breathing causes your belly to expand, not your chest.

- Now start pacing your breath; breathe in slowly for a count of three seconds (one one thousand, two one thousand, three one thousand), hold it in for another three counts, and then breathe out slowly for a final count of three. Feel your thoughts and emotions settling down as you focus on your breath. Be aware that, as you attempt to quiet your mind, thoughts will still come in to pay a visit. Simply acknowledge them and then let them go, always returning your focus to your breath.

- Allow yourself to be fully present in this moment. This is often referred to as "being." Not thinking, not doing, just being. Continue to follow your breath, and imagine inhaling positive, loving, and peaceful energy and exhaling all your worries and stress. Enjoy the quiet. Enjoy the moment. Just breathe…just be.

- If you find that you have a constant influx of thoughts, it may be helpful for you to focus on a single word, phrase, or mantra and repeat it over and over again to yourself as you inhale and exhale. For example, you might try something like this: (On the inhale) "I inhale confidence …" (As you exhale) "I exhale fear …" You can swap the word "confidence" for whatever you feel you need to bring more of into your life (love, faith, energy, etc.), and swap the word "fear" with whatever you feel you need to let go of (stress, worry, resentment, etc.).

Meditation is a gift you can give yourself every day. Our time spent meditating has become one of our favorite parts of the Miracle Morning routine. It's a time to be at peace and to experience gratitude and freedom from day-to-day stressors and worries.

Think of daily meditation as a temporary vacation from your problems. Although your problems will still be there when you finish your daily meditation, you'll find that you're more centered and better equipped to solve them.

A is for Affirmations

Have you ever wondered how some people seem to just be good at *everything* they do and consistently achieve at a level so high, you can hardly comprehend how you're ever going to join them? Or why others seem to drop every ball? Time and time again, it is a person's *mindset* that has proven to be the driving factor in their results.

Mindset can be defined as the accumulation of beliefs, attitude, and emotional intelligence. In her bestselling book, *Mindset: The New Psychology of Success*, Carol Dweck, PhD., states: "For twenty years, my research has shown that the view you adopt of yourself profoundly affects the way you lead your life."

Others can easily sense your mindset. It shows up undeniably in your language, your confidence, and your demeanor. Your mindset affects everything! Show us someone with a successful mindset, and I'll show you a person who is successful in recovery.

We know firsthand, though, how difficult it can be to maintain the right mindset—the confidence, enthusiasm, not to mention motivation—during the roller coaster ride that comes with being in recovery. Mindset is largely something we adopt without conscious thought; at a subconscious level, we have been programmed to think, believe, act, and talk to ourselves a certain way.

Our programming comes from many influences, including what others have told us, what we tell ourselves, and all of our good and bad life experiences. That programming expresses itself in every area of our lives, including the way we behave around our children. And that means, if we want a better family dynamic, we need better mental programming.

Affirmations are a tool for doing just that. They enable you to become more intentional about your goals while also providing the encouragement and positive mindset necessary to achieve them. When you repeatedly tell yourself who you want to be, what you want to accomplish, and how you are going to achieve it, your subconscious mind will shift your beliefs and behavior. Once you believe and act in new ways, you will begin to manifest your affirmations into reality.

Science has proven that affirmations—when done correctly—are one of the most effective tools for quickly becoming the person you need to be to achieve everything you want in your life—for yourself and your family. And yet, affirmations also get a bad rap. Many people have tried them only to be disappointed, with little or no results. However, there is a way to leverage affirmations in a way that will absolutely produce results for you.

By repeatedly articulating and reinforcing to yourself **what** result you want to accomplish, **why** accomplishing it is important to you, **which** specific actions are required to produce that result, and, most importantly—precisely **when** you will commit to taking those actions, your subconscious mind will shift your beliefs and behavior. You'll begin to automatically believe and act in new ways, and eventually manifest your affirmations into your reality. But first…

Why the Old Way of Doing Affirmations Does Not Work

For decades, countless so-called experts and gurus have taught affirmations in ways that have proven to be ineffective and set people up for failure. Here are two of the most common problems with affirmations.

Problem #1: Lying to Yourself Doesn't Work

I am a millionaire. Really?

I have 7 percent body fat. Do you?

I have achieved all of my goals this year. Have you?

Creating affirmations as if you've already become or achieved something may be the single biggest cause of affirmations not being effective for most people.

With this technique, every time you recite the affirmation that isn't rooted in truth, your subconscious will resist it. As an intelligent human being who isn't delusional, lying to yourself repeatedly will never be the optimum strategy. *The truth will always prevail.*

Problem #2: Passive Language Doesn't Produce Results

Many affirmations have been designed to make you feel good by creating an empty promise of something you desire. For example, here is a popular money affirmation that's been perpetuated by many world-famous gurus:

I am a money magnet. Money flows to me effortlessly and in abundance.

This type of affirmation might make you feel good in the moment by giving you a false sense of relief from your financial worries, but it won't generate any income. People who sit back and wait for money to magically show up are cash poor .

To generate the kind of abundance you want (or any result you desire, for that matter), you've got to actually do something. Your actions must be in alignment with your desired results, and your affirmations must articulate and affirm both.

Four Steps to Create Miracle Morning Affirmations (That Produce Results)

Here are the simple steps to create and implement results-oriented Miracle Morning affirmations that will program your conscious and subconscious mind, while redirecting your conscious mind to upgrade your behavior so that you can begin to produce results and take your levels of personal and professional success beyond what you've ever experienced before.

Step One: Identify the Ideal Result You Are Committed to and Why

Notice we're not starting with what you *want*. Everyone wants things, but we don't get what we want: we get what we're committed to. You want to be a great role model for people in recovery? Oh wait, you're 100 percent committed to clarifying and executing the necessary actions until the result is achieved? Okay, now we're talking.

Action: Start by writing down a specific, extraordinary result or outcome—one that challenges you, that would significantly improve your life, and that you are ready to commit to creating—even if you're not yet sure how you will do it. Then reinforce your commitment by including your *why*, the compelling reason you're willing to stay committed.

Examples: *I am dedicated to going on a date night once a week with my significant other to model a healthy love relationship for my children.*

Or …

I am 100 percent committed to being as healthy as I can be so that I have the energy to be fully present with my children and spouse.

Or …

I am committed to doubling my income in the next twelve months, from $50,000 to $100,000, so that I can provide financial security for my family.

Step Two: Name the Necessary Actions You Are Committed to Taking and *When*

Writing an affirmation that merely affirms what you *want* without affirming what you are committed to *doing* is one step above pointless and can be counterproductive by tricking your subconscious mind into thinking that the result will happen automatically, without effort.

Action: Clarify the (specific) action, activity, or habit that is required for you to achieve your ideal outcome, and clearly state when and how often you will execute the necessary action.

Examples: *To ensure I have a date night weekly with my significant other, I am 100 percent committed to lining up a babysitter and choosing an activity by Wednesday of each week for the upcoming weekend, along with blocking that time on my calendar.*

Or …

To ensure that I am as healthy as I can be, I am 100 percent committed to going to the gym five days per week from 6:00 a.m. to 7:00 a.m. and running on the treadmill for a minimum of twenty minutes each day.

Or …

To guarantee that I double my income, I am committed to doubling my daily prospecting calls from twenty to forty calls per day, five days a week, made from 8:00 a.m. to 9:00 a.m.—NO MATTER WHAT .

Or…

To improve my chances of continued recovery, I am committed to attending Twelve-step meetings every day for the next thirty days.

The more specific your actions are, the better. Be sure to include *frequency* (how often), *quantity* (how many), and *precise time frames* (when you will begin and end your activities).

Step Three: Recite Your Affirmations Every Morning (with Emotion)

Remember, your Miracle Morning affirmations aren't designed merely to make you *feel good.* These written statements are strategically engineered to program your subconscious mind with the beliefs and mindset you need to achieve your desired outcomes while directing your conscious mind to keep you focused on your highest priorities and taking the actions that will get you there.

For your affirmations to be effective, however, it is important that you tap into your emotions while reciting them. Mindlessly repeating an affirmation without intentionally feeling its truth will have minimal impact for you. You must take responsibility for generating authentic emotions, such as excitement and determination, and powerfully infusing those emotions in every affirmation you recite.

You must affirm who you need to be to do the things you need to do, so that you can have the results that you want. I'll say this again: it isn't magic; this strategy works when you connect with *the person you need to become* on the way to achieving your goals. It's who you are that attracts your results more than any other activity.

Action: Schedule time each day to read your affirmations during your Miracle Morning to both program your subconscious and focus your conscious mind on what's most important to you and what you are committed to doing to make it your reality. That's right, you must read them daily. Reading your affirmation occasionally is as effective as an occasional workout. You'll start seeing results only when you've made them a part of your daily routine.

A great place to read affirmations is in the shower. If you laminate them and leave them there, then they will be in front of you every day. Put them anywhere you can to remind you: under your car's sun visor, taped to your mirror. The more you see them, the more the subconscious mind can connect with them to change your thinking and your actions. You can even write them directly on a mirror with dry erase markers.

One of Anna's favorite methods is to record herself reading or saying her affirmations into the voice recorder in her phone and then playing them later when she's walking or driving. That way, she gets to hear them over and over again, in her own voice, like she's listening to a motivational speaker—except that motivational speaker is talking specifically about her.

While he doesn't have a formal affirmations practice, Joe will write slogans and quotes on the mirrors in his different bathrooms so he's regularly reminded of them. Sometimes they're 12-step related and sometimes they have to do with pain—about how body pain is actually caused by repressed emotion and not by something structurally wrong. He also keeps art, by a company called Gaping Void, that contains quotes he knows are true but sometimes could benefit from reading or hearing again. His favorite? "Recovery didn't open up the gates of heaven to let me in but it opened up the gates of hell to let me out."

Step Four: Constantly Update and Evolve Your Affirmations

As you continue to grow, improve, and evolve, so should your affirmations. When you come up with a new goal, dream, or extraordinary result you want to create for your life, add it to your affirmations. Any time you come across an empowering quote or philosophy and think to yourself, *Wow, that is an area where I could make a huge improvement,* add it to your affirmations.

Remember, your affirmations should be tailored to you and phrased in the form of "I" statements. They must be specific for them to work in your subconscious.

Your programming can change and improve at any time, starting right now. You can reprogram any perceived limitations with new beliefs and create new behaviors so you can become as successful as you want to be in any area of life you choose.

In summary, your new affirmations articulate the extraordinary results you are committed to creating, why they are critically important to you, and, most importantly, which necessary actions you are committed to taking and when to ensure that you attain and sustain the extraordinary levels of success you truly want (and deserve) for your life.

Affirmations to Become a Level 10 Person in Recovery

In addition to the formula to create your affirmations, we have included this list of sample affirmations, which may help spark your creativity. Feel free to include any of these that resonate with you.

- I am just as worthy, deserving, and capable of achieving a happy life in recovery as any other person on earth, and I will prove that today with my actions.

- Where I am is a result of who I *was*, but where I go depends entirely on who I *choose to be*, starting today.

- I am fully committed to dedicating thirty to sixty minutes each day to do my Miracle Morning and the S.A.V.E.R.S. so that I can continue to become the person I need to be to create everything I want for my life.

- I am fully committed to attending five meetings a week where I will try to be of service to other sober people or volunteering every month at a homeless shelter in order to get out of my own head.

- I will focus on learning new things and improving my recovery skills daily, and I commit to reading or rereading at least one book to help that effort every month.

- I am committed to never-ending improvement in the tasks necessary for my optimal day-to-day functioning.

- I commit to working steps, attending therapy or pursuing a specific form of treatment that may enhance my growth.

- I am committed to reading for twenty minutes every day.

These are just a few examples of affirmations. You can use any that resonate with you, but do create your own, as well, using the four-step formula described in the previous pages. Anything you say repeatedly to yourself with emotion will be programmed into your subconscious mind, help you form new beliefs, and manifest through your actions.

V is for Visualization

Visualization has long been a well-known practice of world-class athletes, who use it to optimize their performance. Olympic athletes and top performers in many categories incorporate visualization as a critical part of their daily training. What is less well known is that successful entrepreneurs—the top achievers—use it just as frequently.

Visualization is a technique in which you use your imagination to create a compelling picture of your future, providing you with heightened clarity and producing the motivation that will assist you in making your vision a reality.

If you'd like some fascinating information about *why* visualization works, just Google "mirror neurons." A neuron is a cell that connects the brain and other parts of the body; a mirror neuron fires when we take an action or observe someone else taking an action. This is a relatively new area of study in neurology, but these cells seem to allow us to improve our abilities by watching other people perform them *or* by visualizing ourselves performing them. Some studies indicate that experienced weight lifters can increase muscle mass through vivid visualization sessions, and mirror neurons get the credit for making this possible. In many ways, the brain can't tell the difference between a vivid visualization and an actual experience. Crazy, right?

What Do You Visualize?

Most anyone is limited by visions of their past results, their minds automatically replaying previous failures and heartbreaks. Creative visualization, on the other hand, enables you to design the vision that will occupy your mind, ensuring that the greatest pull on you is your future.

Since Anna often listens to her recorded affirmations while on a brisk morning walk, as soon as she walks back inside, she does fifty fast jumping jacks while staring at one of her vision boards. Afterwards, she's able to feel the blood pumping through her veins, which makes her feel like she's more than earned the cup of coffee she's about to imbibe.

One thing you don't want to do is visualize the results. Many people will disagree on this, but there are studies that provide scientific evidence showing that merely visualizing the result you want (e.g. the new car, the dream house, crossing the finish line, standing on stage, etc.) can diminish your drive because your brain has already experienced the reward on some level. Instead, we highly recommend focusing your visualization on the necessary actions, more so than just the results. Visualize yourself taking the actions—especially the actions that you habitually resist and procrastinate on—in a way that creates a compelling mental and emotional experience of the action. For example, Hal despised running, but he had made a commitment to himself (and publicly) to run a 52-mile ultra-marathon. Throughout the course of his five months of training, he used Miracle Morning

Visualization to see himself lacing up his running shoes and hitting the pavement—*with a smile on his face and pep in his step*—so that when it was time to train, he had already programmed the experience to be positive and enjoyable.

You might picture yourself at a party where other people are toasting champagne or sipping ice cold beers or at a casino where gamblers are glued to roulette tables and feel how indifferent you are to what they're doing. What does that feel like to be rid of the desire to drink or gamble or act out sexually? Picture yourself shaking your head when someone offers you a glass of Pinot and ordering a club soda with a dash of cranberry and a lime instead. Envision yourself turning away from the casino or strip club.

You can pick anything that is a critical action step or skill that you may not be performing at your best yet. Envisioning success and what it takes to get there will prepare you for, and almost ensure, a successful day.

Three Simple Steps for Miracle Morning Visualization

The perfect time to visualize yourself living in alignment with your affirmations is right after you read them.

Step One: Get Ready

Some people like to play instrumental music in the background during their visualization, such as classical or baroque (check out anything from the composer J. S. Bach). If you'd like to experiment with music, put it on with the volume relatively low.

Now, sit up tall in a comfortable position. This can be on a chair, the couch, or the floor with a cushion. Breathe deeply. Close your eyes, clear your mind, and let go of any self-imposed limitations as you prepare yourself for the benefits of visualization.

Step Two: Visualize What You Really Want

Many people don't feel comfortable visualizing success and are even scared to succeed. Some people may experience resistance in this area.

Some may even feel guilty that they will leave the other 95 percent behind when they become successful.

This famous quote from Marianne Williamson is a great reminder for anyone who feels mental or emotional obstacles when attempting to visualize: "Our deepest fear is not that we are inadequate. Our deepest fear is that we are powerful beyond measure. It is our light, not our darkness that most frightens us. We ask ourselves, 'Who am I to be brilliant, gorgeous, talented, fabulous?' Actually, who are you not to be? You are a child of God. Your playing small does not serve the world. There is nothing enlightened about shrinking so that other people won't feel insecure around you. We are all meant to shine, as children do. We were born to make manifest the glory of God that is within us. It's not just in some of us; it's in everyone. And as we let our own light shine, we unconsciously give other people permission to do the same. As we are liberated from our own fear, our presence automatically liberates others."

Consider that the greatest gift you can give to those you love, and those you lead, is to live to your full potential. What does that look like for you? What do you really want? Forget about logic, limits, and being practical. If you could reach any heights, personally and professionally, what would that look like?

See, feel, hear, touch, taste, and smell every detail of your vision. Involve all your senses to maximize effectiveness. The more vivid you make your vision, the more compelled you'll be to take the necessary actions to make it a reality.

Step Three: Visualize Yourself Taking (and Enjoying) the Necessary Actions

Once you've created a clear mental picture of what you want, begin to see yourself doing precisely what you need to do to achieve your vision, with supreme confidence and enjoying every step of the process. See yourself engaged in the actions you'll need to take (exercising, going to a meeting, working with others, writing, selling, making calls, sending emails, etc.). Picture yourself with a look and *feeling* of supreme confidence as you turn down the offer to meet for Happy Hour or cross the finish line on the 5K you're planning to run.

See and *feel* yourself smiling as you finish the essay you're planning to write about your recovery, filled with a sense of pride for your self-discipline to follow through. In other words, visualize yourself doing what you must do and thoroughly enjoying the process, especially if it's a process you don't naturally enjoy. Imagine what it would look and feel like if you did enjoy it.

Picture the look of determination on your face as you tackle all of the tasks you talked about doing when you were sitting atop bar stools or at the casino or strip club or passing around a mirror lined with drugs—all the "big plans" you were making that were destined to be forgotten about by the next morning, or at least too challenging to attempt with a vicious hangover.

Seeing yourself as the person who has it all together is the first step in actually getting it all together. Imagine yourself joyfully sitting down with your planner and organizing the upcoming days and weeks with appointments and meetings, volunteer work, career accomplishments. Visualize yourself accomplishing all the dreams you gave up on back when you prioritized drinking and doing drugs over everything else.

Final Thoughts on Visualization

When you combine reading your affirmations every morning with daily visualization, you will turbocharge the programming of your subconscious mind for success through peak performance. When you visualize daily, you align your thoughts, feelings, and behaviors with your vision. This makes it easier to maintain the motivation you need to continue taking the necessary actions. Visualization can be a powerful aid in overcoming self-limiting beliefs, as well as self-limiting habits such as procrastination, and get you into the actions necessary to achieve extraordinary results.

E is for Exercise

Exercise should be a staple of your Miracle Morning. Even a few minutes of exercise each day significantly enhances your health, improves your self-confidence and emotional well-being, and enables you to think better and concentrate longer. You'll also notice how quickly your energy increases with daily exercise, and your family will notice it too.

Personal development experts and self-made multimillionaire entrepreneurs Eben Pagan and Tony Robbins both agree that the number one key to success is to start every morning with a personal success ritual. Included in both of their success rituals is some type of morning exercise. Eben articulates the importance of *morning* exercise: "Every morning, you've got to get your heart rate up and get your blood flowing and fill your lungs with oxygen." He continued, "Don't just exercise at the end of the day, or at the middle of the day. And even if you do like to exercise at those times, always incorporate at least ten to twenty minutes of jumping jacks, or some sort of aerobic exercise in the morning." Hey, if it works for Eben and Tony, it will work for us (and you)!

Lest you think you must engage in triathlon or marathon training, think again. Your morning exercise also doesn't need to replace an afternoon or evening regimen if you already have one in place. You can still hit the gym at the usual time. However, the benefits from adding as little as five minutes of morning exercise are undeniable, including improved blood pressure and blood sugar levels and decreased risk of all kinds of scary things like heart disease, osteoporosis, cancer, and diabetes. Maybe most importantly, a little exercise in the morning will increase your energy levels for the rest of the day to help you keep up with your demanding schedule.

You can go for a walk or run, follow along to a yoga video on YouTube, or find a Life S.A.V.E.R.S. buddy and play some early morning racquetball. There's also an excellent app called 7-Minute Workout that gives you a full body workout in—you guessed it—seven minutes. The choice is yours, but pick one activity and do it.

As someone in recovery, you are constantly on the go. You need an endless reserve of energy to make the best of the challenges that come your way, and a daily morning exercise practice is going to provide it.

Exercise for Your Brain

Even if you don't care about your physical health, consider that exercise is simply going to make you smarter and that can only help your problem-solving abilities. Dr. Steven Masley, a Florida physician and nutritionist with a health practice geared toward executives, explains how exercise creates a direct connection to your cognitive ability.

"If we're talking about brain performance, the best predictor of brain speed is aerobic capacity—how well you can run up a hill is very strongly correlated with brain speed and cognitive shifting ability," Masley said.

Masley has designed a corporate wellness program based on the work he's done with more than 1,000 patients. "The average person going into these programs will increase brain speed by 25–30 percent."

Hal chose yoga for his exercise activity and began practicing it shortly after he created the Miracle Morning. He's been doing it and loving it ever since. Our exercise routines differ—and since both of us are inarguably exercise obsessed, we'll get into more thorough discussions about our specific habits later in this book.

Final Thoughts on Exercise

You know that if you want to maintain good health and increase your energy, you must exercise consistently. That's not news to anyone. But what also isn't news is how easy it is to make excuses. Two of the biggest are "I don't have time" and "I'm too tired." And those are just the first two on the list. There is no limit to the excuses you can think of. And the more creative you are, the more excuses you can find!

That's the beauty of incorporating exercise into your Miracle Morning—it happens before your day wears you out and before you have an entire day to come up with new excuses. Because it comes first, the Miracle Morning is a surefire way to avoid those excuses and make exercise a daily habit.

Legal disclaimer: Hopefully this goes without saying, but you should consult your doctor before beginning any exercise regimen, especially if you are experiencing any physical pain, discomfort, disabilities, etc. You may need to modify or even refrain from an exercise routine to meet your individual needs.

R is for Reading

One of the fastest ways to achieve everything you want is to find successful people to be your role models. For every goal you have, there's a good chance an expert out there has already achieved the same thing or something similar. As Tony Robbins says, "Success leaves clues."

Fortunately, some of the best of the best have shared their stories in writing. And that means all those success blueprints are just waiting for anyone willing to invest the time in reading. Books are a limitless supply of help and mentorship right at your fingertips.

If you are already a reader, great! But if up until this point you've been a part of the majority of our society content to clock in and out, putting forth minimal effort for moderate compensation, you have an incredible opportunity here.

Although reading doesn't *directly* produce results (at least not in the short term), there are many activities that can pull us in other, low-level and less fruitful, directions. These benefit us far less in the long run than a consistent reading habit.

Want to flourish in your recovery? Want to learn how to think and grow rich? Ready to awaken the giant within? Be happy for no reason? Implement a four-hour workweek? Double your revenue and profit in three years or less? You're in luck … we've heard that several authors have written books on precisely those topics.

Occasionally, we hear people say, "I'm so busy that I don't have time to read." We get it. But as Hal's mentor used to say: "The greatest minds in human history have spent years condensing the best of what they know into a few pages that can be purchased for a few dollars, read in a few hours, and shorten your learning curve by decades. But I get it … you're too busy." Ouch!

You can find one, ten, or preferably twenty minutes every day to take in valuable content to enrich your life. Just use some of the strategies shared earlier in this book, spend five less minutes on Facebook before you start your day, or read while eating lunch to nourish your mind and body simultaneously.

Here are some books we suggest you start with, and once you've primed your reading pump, we bet you'll keep going and never stop!

On recovery:

- *Clean: Overcoming Addiction & Ending America's Greatest Tragedy* by David Sheff
- *Blackout: Remembering the Things I Drank to Forget* by Sarah Hepola
- *Permanent Midnight* by Jerry Stahl
- *My Lush Sobriety* by Sacha Scoblic
- *Girl Walks into a Bar* by Lisa Smith
- *Codependent No More* by Melodie Beattie
- *Chasing the Scream* by Johann Hari
- *In the Realm of Hungry Ghosts* by Gabor Mate
- *Recovery 2.0* by Tommy Rosen
- *Lit* by Mary Karr
- *The Power of Habit* by Charles Duhigg
- *Party Girl* by Anna David (of course !)

On mindset:

- *The Art of Exceptional Living* by Jim Rohn
- *The One Thing: The Surprisingly Simple Truth Behind Extraordinary Results* by Gary Keller and Jay Papasan
- *The 7 Habits of Highly Effective People: Powerful Lessons in Personal Change* by Stephen R. Covey
- *Mastery* by Robert Greene

- *The 4-Hour Workweek: Escape 9-5, Live Anywhere, and Join the New Rich* by Tim Ferriss
- *The Game of Life and How to Play It* by Florence Scovel Shinn
- *The Compound Effect* by Darren Hardy
- *Taking Life Head On: How to Love the Life You Have While You Create the Life of Your Dreams* by Hal Elrod
- *Think and Grow Rich* by Napoleon Hill
- *Vision to Reality: How Short Term Massive Action Equals Long Term Maximum Results* and *Business Dating: Applying Relationship Rules in Business for Ultimate Success* by Honorée Corder
- *Finding Your Element: How to Discover Your Talents and Passions and Transform Your Life* by Sir Ken Robinson and Lou Aronica
- *Spirit Led Instead: The Little Tool Book of Limitless Transformation* by Jenai Lane

You can also find books on how to transform your relationships, increase your self-confidence, improve your communication skills, learn how to become healthy, and improve any other area of your life you can think of. Head to your library or local bookstore—or do what we do and visit Amazon.com—and you'll find more books than you can possibly imagine on any area of your life you want to improve.

For a complete list of Hal's favorite personal development books—including those that have made the biggest impact on his success and happiness—check out the Recommended Reading list at TMMBook.com.

How Much Should You Read?

We recommend making a commitment to read a minimum of ten pages per day (although five is okay to start with if you read slowly or don't yet enjoy reading).

Ten pages may not seem like a lot, but let's do the math. Reading ten pages a day adds up to 3,650 pages per year, which stacks up to approximately eighteen 200-page books that will enable you to take yourself to the next level so that you can take your success to the next level. All in just ten to fifteen minutes of daily reading, or fifteen to thirty minutes if you read more slowly.

Let us ask you, if you read eighteen personal and/or professional development books in the next twelve months, do you think you'll improve your mindset, gain more confidence, and learn proven strategies that will accelerate your success in recovery? Do you think you'll be a better, more capable version of who you are today? Do you think that will be reflected in your business or career results? Absolutely! Reading ten pages per day is not going to break you, but it will absolutely make you.

Final Thoughts on Reading

Begin with the end in mind—what do you hope to gain from the book? Take a moment to do this now by asking yourself what you want to gain from reading this one.

Books don't have to be read cover to cover, nor do they have to be finished. Remember that this is *your* reading time. Use the table of contents to make sure you are reading the parts you care about most, and don't hesitate to put it down and move to another book if you aren't enjoying it. There is too much incredible information out there to spend any time on the mediocre.

Many Miracle Morning practitioners use their reading time to catch up on their religious texts, such as the Bible or the Torah.

Unless you're borrowing a book from the library or a friend, feel free to underline, circle, highlight, dog-ear, and take notes in the margins of the book. The process of marking books as you read allows you to come back at any time and recapture the key lessons, ideas, and benefits without needing to read the book again cover to cover. If you read on a digital reader, such as Kindle, Nook, or via iBooks, notes and highlighting are easily organized so you can see them each time you flip through the book, or you can go directly to a list of your notes and highlights.

Summarize key ideas, insights, and memorable passages in a journal. You can build your own summary of your favorite books so you can revisit the key content any time in just minutes.

Rereading good personal development books is an underused yet very effective strategy. Rarely can you read a book once and internalize all its value. Achieving mastery in any area requires repetition. Why not try it out with this book? Commit to rereading it as soon as you're finished to deepen your learning and give yourself more time to master your Miracle Morning.

Audiobooks count as reading! You still get the information, and you can do it while exercising or during your commute. When we really want to study a book, we'll listen to the audio while looking at the text. This way we can take notes and underline text without slowing down too much. This is also a way to listen to the audiobook at 1.5 or 2 times the speed and "read" much faster.

Most importantly, quickly implement what you read. Schedule time to implement what you're reading, *while you're reading it.* Literally read with your schedule next to you, and schedule time-blocks to put the content into action. Don't become a personal development junkie who reads a lot but does very little. We've met many people who take pride in the number of books they read, like some badge of honor. We'd rather read and implement one good book than read ten books and then do nothing other than start reading the eleventh book. While reading is a great way to gain knowledge, insights, and strategies, it is the implementation and practice of these new strategies that will advance your life and business. Are you committed to implementing what you're learning in this book by taking action and following through with the 30-Day Challenge at the end?

Glad to hear it. Let's get to the final 'S' of the S.A.V.E.R.S.

S is for Scribing

Scribing is simply another word for writing. Let's keep it real—Hal needed an "S" for the end of S.A.V.E.R.S. because a "W" wouldn't fit anywhere. Thanks, Thesaurus; we owe you one.

The scribing element of your Miracle Morning enables you to write down what you're grateful for and document your insights, ideas, breakthroughs, realizations, successes, and lessons learned, as well as any areas of opportunity, personal growth, or improvement.

Most Miracle Morning practitioners scribe in a journal, for five to ten minutes, during their Miracle Morning. By getting your thoughts out of your head and putting them in writing, you'll immediately gain heightened awareness, clarity, and valuable insights that you'd otherwise be oblivious to.

If you're like Hal used to be, you probably have at least a few half-used and barely touched journals and notebooks. It wasn't until he started his own Miracle Morning practice that scribing quickly became one of his favorite daily habits. As Tony Robbins has said many times, "A life worth living is a life worth recording."

Writing will give you the daily benefits of consciously directing your thoughts, but even more powerful are the insights you'll gain from reviewing your journals, from cover to cover, afterwards—especially at the end of the year.

It is hard to put into words how overwhelmingly constructive the experience of going back and reviewing your journals can be. Michael Maher, *The Miracle Morning for Real Estate Agents* coauthor, is an avid practitioner of the Life S.A.V.E.R.S. Part of Michael's morning routine is to write down his appreciations and affirmations in what he calls his Blessings Book. Michael says it best:

"What you appreciate … APPRECIATES. It is time to take our insatiable appetite for what we want and replace it with an insatiable appetite and gratitude for what we do have. Write your appreciations, be grateful and appreciative, and you will have more of those things you crave—better relationships, more material goods, more happiness."

There is strength in writing down what you appreciate, and reviewing this material can change your mindset on a challenging day. A great practice to add to your routine is to write what you appreciate about your recovery, your significant other, and especially yourself. When we write down the things we appreciate about the people in our lives, even (and particularly) when they are not on their best behavior, it's easier to focus on their positive qualities.

For example, you may be angry with your coworker or friend. Instead of focusing on whatever defect of that person you're judging, work to remember that you, too, have defects and how grateful you are when the people in your life can forgive you and not judge you for them. If someone's late to meet you (Anna lives in LA, where you're still considered "on time" if you arrive less than thirty minutes late), it's easy to get angry, but instead try to feel grateful that the person arrived safely and neither of you got in an accident on the way.

While there are many worthwhile benefits of keeping a daily journal, here are a few more of my favorites. With daily scribing, you'll:

- **Gain Clarity**—Journaling will give you more clarity and understanding of your past and current circumstances and help you work through challenges you're facing, while allowing you to brainstorm, prioritize, and plan your actions each day to optimize your future.

- **Capture Ideas**—You will be able to capture, organize and expand on your ideas and keep from losing the important ones you are saving for an opportune moment in the future.

- **Review Lessons**—Journaling provides a place to record, reference and review the lessons you've learned, from both your wins and any mistakes you make along the way.

- **Acknowledge Your Progress**—Going back and rereading your journal entries from a year—or even a week—ago and seeing how much progress you've made can be hugely beneficial. It truly is one of the most enjoyable, eye-opening, and confidence-inspiring experiences, and it can't be duplicated any other way.

- **Improve Your Memory**—People always think they will remember things, but if you've ever gone to the grocery store without a list, you know this is simply untrue. When we write something down, we are much more likely to remember it, and if we forget, we can always go back and read it again.

Effective Journaling

Here are three simple steps to get started with journaling or improve your current journaling process.

First... Choose a format: physical or digital. You'll want to decide up front if you prefer a traditional, physical journal or a digital journal (on your computer or an app for your phone or tablet). If you aren't sure, experiment with both and see which feels best.

Second... Get a journal. Almost anything can work, but when it comes to a physical journal, there is something to be said for an attractive, durable one that you enjoy looking at—after all, ideally, you're going to have it for the rest of your life. Anna likes to buy Moleskine notebooks while Joe uses an app called Day One on his phone or writes Morning Pages (based on Julia Cameron's recommendation in *The Artist's Way*); all that matters is that you choose what works best for you. Some people prefer journals without lines so they can draw or create mind maps. Others like to have one page for each day of the year that is predated to help them stay accountable.

Here are a few favorite physical journals from TMM Facebook Community:

- *The Miracle Morning Companion Planner* is your hands-on guide for building a happier and more fulfilling life and career. This 12-month, undated planner allows you to start at any time of the year! Incorporating and tracking the Life S.A.V.E.R.S. each day will help you to be more present and intentional in each moment, own every aspect of your day, and to get the most out of your life. Check out a free preview here: MiracleMorning.com/PlannerSample .

- *The Five-Minute Journal* (FiveMinuteJournal.com) has become popular among top performers. It has a very specific format for each day with prompts, such as "I am grateful for ..." and "What would make today great?" It takes five minutes or less and includes an evening option so you can review your day.

- *The Freedom Journal* (TheFreedomJournal.com) gives you a structured daily process that is focused on helping you with a single objective: *Accomplish Your #1 Goal in 100 Days*. Beautifully designed by John Lee Dumas of Entrepreneur On Fire, it's designed specifically to help you set and accomplish one big goal at a time.

- *The Plan: Your Legendary Life Planner* (LegendaryLifePlan. com) was designed by friends of Hal's, and it is a goal-setting and habit-tracking system and planner for people who are ready for life balance and are willing to be intentional about achieving level 10 in all areas of life.

- *The Miracle Morning Journal* (MiracleMorningJournal.com) is designed specifically to enhance and support your Miracle Morning, to keep you organized and accountable, and to track your S.A.V.E.R.S. each day. You can also download a free sample of *The Miracle Morning Journal* today at TMMbook. com to make sure it's right for you.

- If you prefer to use a digital journal, many choices are available. Here are a few favorites:

- *The Five-Minute Journal* (FiveMinuteJournal.com) also offers an iPhone app, which follows the same format as the physical version but allows you to upload photographs to your daily entries and also sends you helpful reminders to input your entries each morning and evening.

- *Penzu* (Penzu.com) is a popular online journal that doesn't require an iPhone, iPad, or Android device. All you need is a computer.

Again, it really comes down to your preference and the features you want. If none of these digital options resonate with you, type "online journal" into Google, or simply type "journal" into the app store, and you'll get a variety of choices.

Third... Scribe daily. There are endless things you can write about—notes from the book you're reading, a list of things you're grateful for, and your top three to five priorities for the day are a good place to start. Write whatever makes you feel good and optimizes your day. Don't worry about grammar, spelling, or punctuation. Your journal is a place to let your imagination run wild; keep a muzzle on your inner critic, and don't edit—just scribe!

Customizing Your S.A.V.E.R.S.

We know that you might have days when you can't do the Miracle Morning practice all at once. Feel free to split up the Life S.A.V.E.R.S. in any way that works for you. Here are a few ideas specifically geared toward customizing the Life S.A.V.E.R.S. based on your schedule and preferences. Your current morning routine might allow you to fit in only a six-, twenty-, or thirty-minute Miracle Morning, or you might choose to do a longer version on the weekends.

Here is an example of a common sixty-minute Miracle Morning schedule using the Life S.A.V.E.R.S.:

- **S**ilence: ten minutes
- **A**ffirmations: five minutes
- **V**isualization: five minutes
- **E**xercise: ten minutes
- **R**eading: twenty minutes
- **S**cribing: ten minutes

You can customize the sequence, too. Anna prefers to start with meditation before moving into affirmations and exercise and then do her reading and writing later in the day, while Joe either meditates first or does a round of burpees (more on this later). Hal prefers to start with a period of peaceful, purposeful silence so that he can wake up slowly, clear his mind, and focus his energy and intentions. However, this is your Miracle Morning, not ours—feel free to experiment with different sequences to see which you like best.

Ego Depletion and Your Miracle Morning

Have you ever wondered why you can resist sugary snacks in the morning, but your resistance crumbles in the afternoon or evening? Why is it that sometimes our willpower is strong and other times it deserts us? It turns out that willpower is like a muscle that grows tired from use, and at the end of the day, it is harder to push ourselves to do activities that serve us and avoid those that don't. It also means we have less patience for our loved ones in the afternoon and evening, when they could probably use it the most.

The good news is that we know how this works and can set ourselves up for success with some advanced planning. And the great news? The Miracle Morning is an integral part of your plan. To see how this works, we need to understand ego depletion.

Ego depletion is a term to describe "a person's diminished capacity to regulate their thoughts, feelings, and actions," according to Roy F. Baumeister and John Tierney, the authors of *Willpower*. Ego depletion grows worse at the end of the day and when we are hungry, tired, or have had to exert our willpower too often.

If you wait until the end of the day to do important things that give you energy and help you become the person you want to be, you'll find that your excuses are more compelling and your motivation has gone missing. But when you wake up and do your Miracle Morning first thing, you gain the increased energy and mindfulness that the Life S.A.V.E.R.S. provide and keep ego depletion from getting in your way.

When you perform the Life S.A.V.E.R.S. habit every day, you learn the mechanics of habit formation when your willpower is strongest, and you can use this knowledge and energy to adopt small and doable habits at other times of the day.

Final Thoughts on the Life S.A.V.E.R.S.

Everything is difficult before it's easy. Every new experience is uncomfortable before it's comfortable. The more you practice the Life S.A.V.E.R.S., the more natural and normal each of them will feel. Hal's first time meditating was almost his last because his mind raced like a Ferrari and his thoughts bounced around uncontrollably like the silver sphere in a pinball machine. Now, he loves meditation, and while he's still no master, he says he's decent at it.

Similarly, Anna had trouble with affirmations when she first started Miracle Mornings. She couldn't stop thinking about Stuart Smalley, the *SNL* character played by comedian-turned-politician Al Franken. Affirmations, she thought, were cheesy! They were for silly people. But then she realized she could be cheesy and silly if it meant feeling better, and what's more, who was she to find something that made her feel better cheesy and silly? That's when she started recording different affirmations for various aspects of her life on her phone—a slew for work, another bunch for her personal life, some for her recovery—and playing them while she did her morning walks around the block.

We invite you to begin practicing the Life S.A.V.E.R.S. now so you can become familiar and comfortable with each of them and get a jump-start before you begin The Miracle Morning 30-Day Challenge in chapter eleven.

The Six-Minute Miracle Morning

If your biggest concern is still finding time, don't worry; we've got you covered. You can do the entire Miracle Morning—receiving the full benefits of all six S.A.V.E.R.S.—in only six minutes a day, literally. While six minutes isn't the duration we'd recommend on an ongoing basis, for those days when you're pressed for time, simply do each of the S.A.V.E.R.S., for one minute each:

- **Minute One (S):** Close your eyes and enjoy a moment of peaceful, purposeful silence to clear your mind and get centered for your day.

- **Minute Two (A):** Read your most important affirmation to reinforce *what* result you want to accomplish, *why* it's important to you, *which* specific actions you must take, and most importantly—precisely *when* you will commit to taking those actions

- **Minute Three (V):** Visualize yourself flawlessly executing the single most important action that you want to accomplish for the day.

- **Minute Four (E):** Stand up and engage in some high-energy jumping jacks, or drop and do push-ups and/or crunches, to get your heart rate up and engage your physiology.

- **Minute Five (R):** Grab the book you're reading and read a page or a paragraph, and finally…

- **Minute Six (S):** Grab your journal, and jot down one thing that you're grateful for, along with the single most important result for you to generate that day.

We're sure you can see how, even in just six minutes, the S.A.V.E.R.S. will set you on the right path for the day—and you can always devote more time later when your schedule permits or the opportunity presents itself. Doing the six-minute practice is a way to start a mini habit to build up your confidence or a way to bookmark the habit on a tough morning. Another mini habit you could do is to start with one of the Life S.A.V.E.R.S., and, once you get used to waking up earlier, add more of them. Remember that the goal is to have some time to work on your personal goals and mindset, so if you are overwhelmed, it's not going to work for you.

Personally, our Miracle Mornings have grown into daily rituals of renewal and inspiration that we absolutely love. In the coming chapters, we will cover *a lot* of information that has the potential to turn you into a truly confident person in recovery, and we can't wait to share it with you.

RECOVERY WARRIOR MIRACLE MORNING ROUTINE

RYAN HAMPTON
FACEBOOK.COM/ADDICTIONXAMERICA
TWITTER: @RYANFORRECOVERY
INSTAGRAM: @RYANJHAMPTON

Three years into recovery from a decade-long heroin addiction, Ryan Hampton has been rocketed to the center of America's rising recovery advocacy movement. He is now a prominent, leading face and voice of addiction recovery and is changing the national dialog about addiction through social media. With content that reaches over one million people a week, Ryan is breaking down cultural barriers that have kept people suffering in silence and is inspiring a digital revolution of people recovering out loud through his #VoicesProject. He's also advocating for solutions and holding public policymakers accountable. He was part of the core team that released the first-ever U.S. Surgeon General's report on addiction and was singled out by *Forbes* as a top social media entrepreneur in the recovery movement. Ryan connects a vast network of people who are passionate about ending the drug epidemic in America. His writing on recovery- and addiction-related issues regularly go viral in online journals such as *HuffPost* and *The Hill*. He also serves as an outreach lead and recovery activist for Facing Addiction, America's leading non-profit dedicated to ending the addiction crisis in the United States. In 2016, Ryan created the web series *Facing Addiction Across America*, documenting his thirty-day, twenty-eight-state, 8,000-mile cross-country trip visiting areas hit hardest by the addiction crisis.

Ryan's morning routine:

- I always wake up between 5 a.m. and 6:15 a.m.
- I find tremendous peace in waking up early and getting my day started without interruption.

- Before I do anything, I make my bed. If my bed isn't made, my mind isn't clear. I know it sounds weird—but I feel like I'm off to a good start if my bed is tidy before beginning my day.

- I then say "good morning" to my dog; he usually gets the next five minutes of my morning before I make coffee or grab an Absolute Zero energy drink, gather my headphones and iPhone, and walk downstairs to the outside courtyard in my complex.

- Between 6:30 a.m. to 7:30 a.m., I do nothing but listen to music and think about the day ahead. I try not to respond to emails or take phone calls during this time. Some people meditate—I listen to music; it's my form of meditation.

- By this time (usually around 7:30 a.m.), my head is pretty clear, and I'm almost ready to start my day. I head back up to my apartment, check my vision board (which I update on the daily), check what tasks I have ahead of me, add any new ones, pop open my laptop to return any emails that arrived overnight, check my daily calendar, and by 8:15 a.m., I'm off to the gym for thirty minutes of cardio.

- This usually gets me back home by 9 a.m., which is when I take a quick shower, get dressed, and *officially* begin my day.

- When I follow this routine, I feel like I'm in a forward-moving, level-headed position for my day.

SECTION II:

THE NOT-SO-OBVIOUS RECOVERY PRINCIPLES

— 4 —

NOT-SO-OBVIOUS RECOVERY PRINCIPLE #1:

SELF-LEADERSHIP

"Your level of success will seldom exceed your level of personal development… because success is something you attract by the person you become."
—JIM ROHN

"You better lose yourself in the music, the moment. You own it, you better never let it go…"
—EMINEM

We've been lied to. Yep. Society has conditioned all of us to think that the only way to *have* more is to *do* more.

Want more money? Work harder. Put in *more* hours.

Want more sex? Lift *more* weight and log *more* steps in your Fitbit.

Want more love? Do *more* for your partner than they do for you.

But what if the real secret to having more of what we want in our lives is not about *doing* more but rather *becoming* more.

It is this philosophy that gave birth to, and remains the foundation of, the Miracle Morning: that our levels of success *in every single area of our lives* is always determined by our levels of *personal development* (i.e. our beliefs, knowledge, emotional intelligence, skills, abilities, faith, etc.). So, if we want to have more, we must first become more.

Think of it this way: if you were to measure your desired level of success, on a scale of one to ten, in every area of your life, it's safe to say that you want "level 10" success in each area. We've never met anyone who honestly said, *"Nah, I don't want to be too happy... too healthy... or too wealthy... I am content just settling for less than my potential and cruising along with a level 5 life."*

But what are we doing each day to first become a level 10 person?

In other words, who you're becoming is far more important than what you're doing, and yet the irony is that what you're doing, each day, is determining who you're becoming.

Andrew Bryant, founder of Self-Leadership International, summed it up this way: "Self-leadership is the practice of intentionally influencing your thinking, feeling, and behaviors to achieve your objective(s) ... [It] is having a developed sense of who you are, what you can do, and where you are going coupled with the ability to influence your communication, emotions, and behaviors on the way to getting there."

Before we reveal the key principles of self-leadership, we want to share with you what we've discovered about the crucial role that *mindset* plays as the foundation of effective self-leadership. Your past beliefs, self-image, and the ability to collaborate with and rely upon others at integral times will factor into your ability to excel as a self-leader.

Be Aware of—and Skeptical of—Your Self-Imposed Limitations

You may be holding on to false limiting beliefs that are unconsciously interfering with your ability to achieve your personal and professional goals.

For example, you may be someone who repeats, "I wish I were more organized." Yet you are more than capable of providing the structure and inspiration to be organized. Thinking of yourself as less-than-capable assumes imminent failure and simultaneously thwarts your ability to succeed. Life contains enough obstacles without your creating more for yourself!

Effective self-leaders closely examine their beliefs, decide which ones serve them, and eliminate the ones that don't.

When you find yourself stating anything that sounds like a limiting belief, from "I don't have enough time" to "I could never do that," pause and turn your self-limiting statements into empowering questions, such as the following: *Where can I find more time in my schedule? How might I be able to do that?*

Doing this allows you to tap into your inborn creativity and find solutions. You can always find a way when you're committed. As tennis star Martina Navratilova said, "The difference between involvement and commitment is like ham and eggs. The chicken is involved; the pig is committed." Being all in is the key to making anything happen.

See Yourself as Better than You've Ever Been

As Hal wrote in *The Miracle Morning*, most of us suffer from Rearview Mirror Syndrome, limiting our current and future results based on who we were in the past. Remember that, although *where you are is a result of who you were, where you go depends entirely on the person you choose to be from this moment forward.* This is especially important for people in recovery. You will make mistakes. Don't let your sense of guilt about that keep you from looking forward. Learn from your mistakes, and do better next time.

Sara Blakely, the founder of Spanx and the youngest self-made female billionaire in the United States, once said in an interview that she attributes her success to a mindset her father instilled in her. "When I was growing up, he encouraged us to fail. We'd come home from school and at dinner he'd say: 'What did you fail at today?' And if there was nothing, he'd be disappointed. It was an interesting kind of reverse psychology. I would come home and say that I tried out for something and I was just horrible and he high-fived me." Our mistakes can turn into our greatest lessons, if we allow them to.

We all make mistakes! As human beings, we do not come with instruction manuals, and there will always be someone with an unsolicited opinion about the way you are living your life. Don't listen to the static! Be confident in your choices, and when you aren't sure, find the answers and support you need.

All successful people, at some point, made the choice to see themselves as better than they had ever been before. They stopped maintaining limiting beliefs based on their past and instead started forming beliefs based on their unlimited potential.

One of the best ways to do this is to follow the four-step Miracle Morning Affirmations formula for creating results-oriented affirmations, as outlined in the last chapter. Be sure to create affirmations that reinforce what's possible for you by reminding you of your ideal outcome, why it's important to you, which actions you're committed to taking to achieve it, and precisely when you're committed to taking those actions.

Actively Seek Support

Seeking support is crucial for people in recovery, yet many struggle, suffering in silence because they assume everyone else has greater capabilities, and they all but refuse to seek help and assistance.

People who are self-leaders know they can't do it alone. You might need moral support, for example, so you can replenish the energy stores that life is so famous for depleting. Or you may need accountability support to overcome your tendency to disengage when the going gets tough. We all need support in different areas of our lives, and great self-leaders understand that and use it to their benefit.

The Miracle Morning Community on Facebook is a great place to start looking for support. The members are positive and responsive. Try joining a local group for people with similar goals and interests. Meetup.com is a great place to find like-minded folks who are close by. We highly recommend getting an accountability partner and, if you can, a life or business coach to help you.

The Five Foundational Principles of Self-Leadership

While self-leadership is a skill, all skills are built on a foundation of principles. To grow and reach the levels of success you aspire to reach, you'll need to become a proficient self-leader. Our favorite way to cut the learning curve in half and decrease the time it takes for you to reach the top one percent is to model the traits and behaviors of those who have reached the top before you.

During our years of recovery, we've seen many leaders and a myriad of effective strategies. Here are the five principles we believe will make the biggest impact on your commitment to self-leadership:

1. Take 100 Percent Responsibility
2. Prioritize Fitness and Make Exercise Enjoyable
3. Aim for Financial Freedom
4. Systematize Your World
5. Commit to Your Result-Producing Process

Principle #1: Take 100 Percent Responsibility

Here's the hard truth: if your life is not where you want it to be, it's all on you.

The sooner you take ownership of that fact, the sooner you'll begin to move forward. This isn't meant to be harsh. Successful people are rarely victims. In fact, one of the reasons they are successful is that they take absolute, total, and complete responsibility for each and every single aspect of their lives—whether it's personal or professional, good or bad, their job or someone else's.

While victims habitually waste their time and energy blaming others and complaining, achievers are busy creating the results and circumstances they want for their lives.

Hal has articulated a profound distinction during one of his keynote speeches: "The moment you take 100 percent responsibility for everything in your life is the same moment you claim your power to change anything in your life. However, the crucial distinction is to realize that taking responsibility is not the same thing as accepting *blame*. While blame determines who is at fault for something, responsibility determines who is committed to improving a situation. It rarely matters who is at fault. All that matters is that YOU are committed to improving your situation." He's right. And it's so empowering when you truly start to think and act accordingly. Suddenly, your life—and your results—are within your control.

When you take true ownership of your life, there's no time for discussing whose fault something is, or who gets the blame. Playing the blame game is easy, but there's no longer any place for it in your life. Finding reasons why you didn't meet your goals is for the other guy, not you. You own your results—good and bad. You can celebrate the good, and learn from the so-called bad. Either way, you always have a choice about how you respond or react in any and every situation.

One of the reasons this mindset is so important is that you are leading by example. If you're always looking for someone to blame, your team sees that, and they likely don't respect it. Like a parent trying to bring out the best in their kids, the people you lead are always watching you, and it's crucial to live by the values that you want to instill in each of them.

Here's the psychological shift we suggest you make: take ownership and stewardship over all of your decisions, actions, and outcomes, starting right now. Replace unnecessary blame with unwavering responsibility. Even if someone else drops that ball, ask yourself what you could have done and, more importantly, what you can do in the future to prevent that ball from being dropped. While you can't change what's in the past, the good news is that you can change everything else.

From now on, there's no doubt about who is at the wheel and who is responsible for all of your results. You make the calls, do the follow-up, decide the outcomes you want, and achieve the goals. Your results are 100 percent your responsibility. Right?

Remember: you are in the position of power, you are in control, and there are no limits to what you can accomplish.

Principle #2: Prioritize Fitness and Make Exercise Enjoyable

On a scale of one to ten, where would you rank your health and fitness? Are you fit? Strong? Do you *feel* good, more often than not?

How about your energy level throughout the day? Do you have more energy than you know what to do with? Can you wake up before your alarm and do what's important, handle all the demands of the day, and put out the inevitable fires, all without struggling to make it through the day without feeling exhausted and out of breath?

We covered exercise as the "E" in S.A.V.E.R.S., and yes, we're going to discuss it again right now. It's a fact that the state of your health and fitness is a huge factor in your energy and success levels. Like any sport, you need an extraordinary supply of energy and stamina.

It's no surprise, then, that three priorities of top performers, each of which you must prioritize in your life, are the quality of their food, their sleep, and their exercise. We'll delve deeper into each in the next chapter on energy engineering, but let's start with making sure you get your daily exercise in, and the key is to find physical activities that you truly enjoy doing.

Make exercise enjoyable. The correlation between physical fitness, happiness, and success is undeniable. It is no coincidence that you rarely see top performers who are terribly out of shape. Most schedule and invest thirty to sixty minutes of their time each day to hit the gym or the running trail, because they understand the important role that daily exercise plays in their success.

While the "E" in S.A.V.E.R.S. ensures that you're going to start each day with five to ten minutes of exercise, we recommended that you make a commitment to engage in additional thirty- to sixty-minute workouts, at least three to five times per week. Doing so will ensure that your fitness level supports the energy and confidence you need to succeed.

Even better is to engage in some form of exercise that brings you a deep level of enjoyment. That might mean going for a hike in nature, playing ultimate Frisbee, or getting an exercise bike and putting it in front of your TV so you can enjoy your favorite episode of *Breaking*

Bad and forget that you're even exercising. Or, do what Hal does; he loves wakeboarding and playing basketball—two excellent forms of exercise—so he does one of them, every single workday. You'll see Hal's foundational schedule in the coming pages, so you know how those activities fit with the rest of his priorities.

Which physical activities do you enjoy, that you can commit to scheduling as part of your daily exercise ritual?

Principle #3: Aim for Financial Freedom

How is your journey toward financial freedom looking? Are you debt-free? Are you on pace for financial freedom? If so, congratulations. You are among a very small percentage of people who are genuinely thriving with their finances.

If not, you're not alone. Most people have less than $10,000 to their name and an average of $16,000 in unsecured debt. No judgment here if your finances are not yet where you want them to be; we're simply going to point you right back to principle one and encourage you to take 100 percent responsibility for your financial situation.

We've seen and heard every reason for someone to dive deep into debt, fail to save, and not have a nest egg. None of those matter now. Yes, the best time to have started saving a percentage of your income was five, ten, or even twenty years ago. But the next best time is right now. Whether you're twenty, forty, sixty, or eighty years old, it's never too late to take control of your personal finances. You'll find an incredible boost in energy from taking charge, and you'll be able to use your accumulated savings to create even more wealth because you'll have money to invest in new opportunities. Sounds good, right?

Financial freedom isn't something you achieve overnight. It is a result of developing the mindset and the habits *now* that will take you down the path that leads to financial freedom. Here are 4.8 practical steps you can start taking today to ensure that you are aiming your financial habits toward a future of financial freedom:

1.0 Set aside 10 percent of your income to save and invest.

This is a must. In fact, we recommend that you start by taking 10 percent of whatever funds you have in the bank right now and putting it into a separate savings account. (Go ahead, we'll wait.) Make whatever adjustments you need to make to your lifestyle to be able to live off of 90 percent of your current income. A little discipline and sacrifice goes a long way. Seeing that 10 percent add up over time gets exciting, and you'll start to *feel* what's possible for the future.

2.0 Take another 10 percent and give it away.

Most wealthy people give a percentage of their income to causes they believe in. But you don't have to wait until you're wealthy to start this practice. Tony Robbins said, "If you won't give $1 out of $10, you'll never give $1 million out of $10 million." Can't do 10 percent or the rent check will bounce? Fine, start with 5, 2, or 1 percent. It's not the amount that matters but rather developing the mindset and creating the habit that will change your financial future and serve you for the rest of your life. You've got to start teaching your subconscious brain that it can produce an abundant income, that there's more than enough, and that there is always more on the way.

3.0 Continuously develop your money mindset.

It's one of the most important topics for you to master, and you can start by adding the following books, which cover various aspects of financial freedom, to your reading list:

- *Profit First: A Simple System to Transform Any Business from a Cash-Eating Monster to a Money-Making Machine* by Mike Michalowicz

- *Secrets of the Millionaire Mind: Mastering the Inner Game of Wealth* by T. Harv Ecker

- *The Magic Money Books 1-3: A Course in Creating Abundance* by Holly Alexander

- *The Total Money Makeover: A Proven Plan for Financial Fitness* by Dave Ramsey
- *The Millionaire Fastlane: Crack the Code to Wealth and Live Rich for a Lifetime* by MJ DeMarco
- *MONEY: Master the Game: 7 Simple Steps to Financial Freedom* by Anthony Robbins
- *Think and Grow Rich* by Napoleon Hill
- *Rich Dad Poor Dad* by Robert Kiyosaki

4.0 Diversify Your Sources of Income.

Creating one or more additional streams of income is no longer a luxury. In today's unpredictable economy, it has become important.

Diversifying your sources of income, also known as *creating multiple streams of income*, is one of the best decisions you can make. It is crucial to not only protect yourself and your family against the unavoidable ups and downs of economic and industry cycles but to establish a lifetime of financial independence. Due to the financial risks that come from relying on ONE source of income, such as a job or even a business, we highly recommend beginning to focus on creating at least one or more additional sources to generate cash flow.

At the age of twenty-five, Hal began planning his exit strategy to leave a lucrative hall of fame sales career to pursue his dream of becoming a full-time entrepreneur. While retaining his sales position and the income it generated, he started his first business. Also his first additional stream of income, he provided sales coaching for both individual sales reps and sales teams. When the economy crashed in 2008, Hal's income was almost entirely dependent on his coaching business. When more than half of his clients couldn't afford to pay for his coaching and he lost over half of his income, he swore he'd never be dependent on one source of income again.

Year by year, using the exact step-by-step formula outlined below, Hal has since added nine additional, significant streams of income. These still include private coaching, as well as running group coaching programs, writing books, presenting keynote speeches , facilitating paid masterminds, podcasting, foreign publishing, franchising and publishing books in *The Miracle Morning* book series, growing affiliate income, and hosting live 300+ person events.

Your additional income streams can be active, passive or a combination of the two. Some may pay you for engaging in work that you love (active), while others can provide income for you without you having to do much of anything at all (passive). You can diversify your income streams among different industries to protect yourself against major losses during downturns in one market and allow you to financially benefit from the upswings in another.

And while Hal's approach to creating multiple streams of income, mentioned above and outlined below, is just one of countless that you could take (i.e. you could buy real estate, leverage the stock market, open brick-and-mortar storefronts, etc.), the following steps (4.1-4.2) give you a practical, straightforward process, which you can begin brainstorming and implementing immediately.

What's important is that you make diversifying your sources of income a priority. Schedule time-blocks in your schedule—one hour per day, one day per week, or a few hours every Saturday—so that you can begin to establish additional income sources that bring you supplemental monthly income, which will provide financial security in the present and ultimately financial freedom in the as-soon-as-possible future. Here are the eight steps that Hal has repeatedly implemented, which you can apply or modify to fit your situation:

4.1 Establish financial security.

Now, this step isn't sexy, but it's imperative. You might think of it as a disclaimer. Don't focus your time and energy into building a *second* source of income until your *primary* source is secure. Whether you have a day job or own a business, focus on establishing and securing a primary monthly income that will support your expenses before you pursue other steps. In other words, don't "burn the ships" like Cortés, until you've at least established a row boat that will keep you afloat while you're building your yacht.

4.2 Clarify your unique value.

Every person on this planet has unique gifts, abilities, experiences and value to offer in a way that benefits others and for which they can be highly compensated. Figure out the knowledge, experience, ability or solution you have or can create, which others will find value in, and think about a way to get them to pay you for it. Remember, what might be common knowledge to you isn't for other people. Here are a few ways that you can differentiate your value in the marketplace.

First... *who you are* and your unique personality will always differentiate your value from that of every other person on earth. Many people will resonate with your personality better than they will with someone else who's offering value that's similar or even the same.

Second... *knowledge* is the one thing you can increase relatively quickly. As Tony Robbins wrote in *Money: Master the Game,* "One reason people succeed is that they have knowledge other people don't have. You pay your lawyer or your doctor for the knowledge and skills you lack."

Increasing your knowledge in a specific area is an effective way to increase the value that others will pay you for—either to teach them what you know, or to apply your knowledge on their behalf.

Third... *packaging* is how you can differentiate your value. When Hal wrote *The Miracle Morning*, he admittedly had to overcome his insecurity around the fact that waking up early wasn't exactly something he invented. He wondered, would there really be a market for the book? But as hundreds of thousands of readers have shared, what made the book so impactful is the way that the information was packaged. It was simple, and it gave people a step-by-step process that made it possible for anyone to significantly improve any area of their life by simply altering how they start their day.

Principle #4: Systematize Your World

Effective people in recovery have *systems* for just about everything, from work activities—such as scheduling, follow-up, entering orders, and sending thank-you cards— to personal activities—such as sleeping, eating, going to meetings, meditating, and taking care of family responsibilities. Those systems make life easier and ensure those in recovery are ready for anything.

Here are a few practices you can implement immediately to begin systematizing your world:

1. Automation

If you find something in your life that does not bring you joy, try to eliminate it through automation. For instance, constantly needing to stop at the grocery store for replenishments can become burdensome, so some people use services that deliver groceries.

Many of us hate cleaning toilets and doing the laundry. If it's possible, we recommend finding a way to hire help for those chores. One benefit of that is that it makes us accountable for keeping the house clutter-free. The housekeepers can do their job well only if things are up off the floor and surfaces. We realize housekeepers may not be in the budget for everyone, but if you can't yet afford one, you may be able to trade services with friends or come up with other creative solutions. One of Hal's friends includes house cleaning as the exercise portion of the Life S.A.V.E.R.S., so a little gets done every morning.

2. Briefcases and Beyond

Hal, in addition to being a best-selling author, is a speaker who travels week after week, sharing *The Miracle Morning* message with audiences around the country and abroad. Collecting the items he needed for every trip was time-consuming, inefficient, and ineffective because he would often forget something at home or in his office. After the third time he forgot the charger for his computer and had to find an Apple store to buy a $99 replacement (ouch) or ask the front desk for a phone charger, shaver, or an extra set of cufflinks left behind by a previous guest, he'd had enough. He assembled a travel bag containing every item he needs for his trips, and now he can leave at a moment's notice because his bag contains everything to conduct business on the road: business cards, brochures, copies of his books, adapters, and chargers for his phone and computer. He even includes earplugs in case his hotel room neighbor is noisy.

You'll know you need a system when you have a recurring challenge or find that you're missing important items because you're unprepared. If you're walking out the door with just enough time to get to your first destination of the day on schedule only to discover your car is running on fumes, you need a system for getting out the door earlier. Here are some ways to plan ahead:

- pack your lunch, your purse or briefcase, and your gym bag the night before, and lay out your outfit for the next day

- prepare an out-of-office kit with brochures, catalogs, or other items you need when traveling for business

- stash healthy snacks for when you're on the go (apples, kale chips, carrots, etc.) to prevent stopping at a convenience store or fast food joint for a not-so-healthy option

Said another way, wherever you need to get your act together, you need a system. A life without systems is a life with unnecessary stress! This is especially true for busy people in recovery.

3. Foundational Scheduling

The use of a foundational schedule is key to maximizing your focus, productivity, and recovery. If we spend too many days bouncing around from one task to another and end far too many days wondering where in the hell the time went and what, if any, significant progress was made, we've missed more key opportunities than we can calculate. Can you relate?

We're going to share—or at least remind you of—something that will transform your ability to produce consistent and spectacular results. *Creating a foundational schedule that gives structure and intentionality to your days and weeks will make your life indescribably easier.* A foundational schedule is a predetermined, recurring schedule that is made up of focused time-blocks, which are each dedicated to your highest-priority activities. Most of us intuitively understand the benefits of this, but very few do it effectively on a consistent basis.

We know—you became an adult to get away from structure. Trust us, we get it. But the more you leverage a foundational schedule, consisting of time-blocks—typically ranging from one to three hours each—that are dedicated to focusing on the projects or activities that will help you make the most of your life and business—the more freedom you'll ultimately create.

That's not to say you cannot have flexibility in your schedule. In fact, we strongly suggest that you *schedule* flexibility. Plan plenty of time-blocks for family, fun, and recreation into your calendar. You could even go as far as to include a "whatever I feel like" time-block, during which you do, well ... whatever you feel like. You can also move things on occasion as needed. What's important is that you go through your days and weeks with a high level of clarity and intentionality with regard to how you're going to invest every hour of every day, even if that hour is spent doing *whatever you feel like*. At least you planned on it. Maintaining a foundational schedule is how you will ensure that you maximize your productivity, so that you almost never end the day wondering where in the hell your time went. It won't go anywhere without you making a conscious decision, because you'll be intentional with every minute of it.

We asked Hal to share his weekly foundational schedule, so you can see an example. Although Hal has the luxury of entrepreneurial freedom and doesn't need to follow any predetermined schedule, he will tell you that having this foundational schedule in place is one of his keys to ensuring he maximizes each day.

Keep in mind that, as happens to most everyone, things come up that cause Hal's foundational schedule to change (events, speaking engagements, vacations, etc.), but only temporarily. As soon as he's back home, and in his office, this is the schedule that he falls back into.

HAL'S FOUNDATIONAL SCHEDULE

Time	Mon	Tues
4:00 AM	SAVERS	SAVERS
5:00 AM	Write	Write
6:00 AM	Emails	Emails
7:00 AM	Take kids to school	Take kids to school
8:00 AM	Staff Mtg.	#1 Priority
9:00 AM	#1 Priority	Wakeboard
⬇	⬇	⬇
11:00 AM	Lunch	Lunch
12:00 PM	Basketball	Priorities
1:00 PM	Priorities	Interview
2:00 PM	Priorities	Interview
3:00 PM	Priorities	Interview
4:00 PM	Priorities	Priorities
5:00 PM	FAMILY	FAMILY
⬇	⬇	⬇
10:00 PM	Bed	Bed

(Note: Every hour is planned.)

Wed	Thurs	Fri	Sat/Sun
SAVERS	SAVERS	SAVERS	SAVERS
Write	Write	Write	Write
Emails	Emails	Emails	↓
Take kids to school	Take kids to school	Take kids to school	FAMILY Time
#1 Priority	#1 Priority	#1 Priority	↓
↓	Wakeboard	↓	↓
↓	↓	↓	↓
Lunch	Lunch	Lunch	↓
Basketball	Priorities	Basketball	↓
Client Call	Interview	Priorities	↓
Client Call	Interview	Priorities	↓
Client Call	Interview	Priorities	↓
Priorities	Priorities	PLANNING	↓
FAMILY	FAMILY	Date Night	↓
↓	↓	↓	↓
Bed	Bed	:^) ???	Bed

One of the main reasons this technique is so effective is that it takes the emotional roller coaster, caused by varied results, out of the decision-making for your daily activities. How many times has an appointment gone wrong and then affected your emotional state and your ability to focus? Chances are, your focus and productivity were hindered for the rest of that day. If you had followed your foundational schedule, though, and the calendar said networking event, writing ads, or making calls, and you were committed to the calendar, then you would have had a fruitful afternoon. Take control. Stop leaving your productivity up to chance and letting outside influences manage your calendar. Create your foundational schedule—one that incorporates everything you need to get done, as well as recreational, family and fun time—and follow through with it, no matter what.

If you find you need additional support to ensure that you follow through, send a copy of your foundational schedule to an accountability partner or your coach, and have them hold you accountable. Your commitment to this one system will allow you to have significantly more control over your productivity and results.

Principle #5: Commit to Consistency

If there is any not-so-obvious secret to success, this is it: *commit to consistency*. Every result that you desire—from improving your physique to increasing the size of your business to spending more quality time with your family—requires a consistent approach to produce the desired results.

In the chapters that follow, we'll give you the insight and direction you need to take consistent action. For now, prepare your mind to keep going—even when the results you want aren't coming fast enough—and to have the stamina to withstand plenty of rejection and disappointment as you adjust to your new self. The most fulfilled people in recovery are often consistent, persistent, and unfailing in their dedication to taking action every day, and you can be the same!

How is your self-esteem doing?

As American playwright August Wilson suggests, "Confront the dark parts of yourself, and work to banish them with illumination and forgiveness. Your willingness to wrestle with your demons will cause your angels to sing." Self-esteem gives you the courage to try new things and the power to believe in yourself.

It is vitally important that you give yourself permission to feel proud of yourself. Yes, we need to be realistic about our weaknesses and always strive to improve, but don't hesitate to be proud of your strengths and revel in the little wins. In the meantime, many days are filled with disappointments, delays, and denials, so it is vitally important that you love yourself. If you are doing the best you can, give yourself credit. Hal actually keeps a special section in his journal to write love notes to himself. On days he needs a little extra encouragement, he writes down all the things he loves and appreciates about himself. On nights when Anna notes the character defects she feels she's acted on in a given day, she also makes sure to remember those things she did well—whether that was having smiled at every stranger she saw or been of service to other people.

An unstoppable self-esteem is a powerful tool. You probably already know that with a negative attitude you are going nowhere—and fast! With the right attitude, all the challenges of the day can roll off your back. You stay calm and can keep going. When you are confident in your abilities and committed to consistency, your behavior will change, and your success is inevitable.

Putting Self-Leadership into Action

Let's review the concepts we discussed in this chapter. We talked about the importance of self-leadership in improving your life, both personally and professionally. Developing self-leadership helps put you in the leadership role of your life. It eliminates the victim mentality and ensures you know the values, beliefs, and vision you want to live into.

Step One: Review and integrate the Five Foundational Principles of Self-Leadership:

1. **Take 100 Percent Responsibility.** Remember, the moment you accept responsibility for *everything* in your life is the moment you claim the power to change *anything* in your life. Your success is 100 percent up to you.

2. **Prioritize Fitness and Make Exercise Enjoyable.** If daily fitness isn't already a priority in your life, make it so. In addition to your morning exercise, block time for longer, thirty- to sixty-minute workouts three to five times each week. As for which foods will give you a surplus of energy, we'll cover that in the next chapter.

3. **Aim for Financial Freedom.** Begin to develop the mindset and habits that will inevitably lead you to a life of financial freedom, including saving a minimum of 10 percent of your income, continuously educating yourself on the topic of money, and diversifying your sources of income.

4. **Systematize Your World.** Start by creating a foundational schedule, and then identify which area of your life or business can benefit by you putting systems and time-blocked schedules in place so that every day your result-producing processes have been predetermined and your success is virtually guaranteed. Most importantly, make sure you instill some system for accountability into your world, whether that be through a colleague or a coach, or by leveraging your team by making commitments to them and leading by example.

5. **Commit to Consistency.** Everyone needs structure. Choose consistency and commit to personal expectations and values. If you're trying a new approach, give it an extended period to work before throwing in the towel to try something different.

Step Two: Develop your self-control and upgrade your self-image by using affirmations and visualization. Be sure to customize both at your earliest opportunity—it takes time to see results, and the sooner you start, the sooner you'll notice improvements.

By now, we hope you've gained a sense of how important your personal development is in creating success. As you continue to read this book—and we suggest you read it more than once—we recommend that you intentionally address the areas where you know you need improvement and expansion. If your self-esteem could use a boost, then take steps to elevate it. Design affirmations to increase and develop it over time. Visualize yourself acting with more confidence, raising your personal standards, and loving yourself more.

If this sounds overwhelming, remember the power of incremental change. You don't have to do everything all at once. And, we've got more good news for you. In the next chapter, we're going to break down exactly how to engineer your life to create optimum levels of sustained physical, mental, and emotional energy so that you're able to maintain extraordinary levels of clarity, focus, and action, day in and day out.

RECOVERY WARRIOR MORNING ROUTINE

PATTY POWERS
FACEBOOK.COM/PATTYPOWERS.SOBERCOACH
TWITTER/INSTAGRAM: @SOBERCOACHNYC

Patty Powers is a nationally recognized certified recovery coach and writer living in New York City. She has been clean and sober since 1988.

Patty's morning routine:

- I usually wake up between 7:30 and 9 a.m. (whatever provides me with six to eight hours of sleep). I set my alarm clock in the next room to force me out of bed.

- I start making coffee right away and running a bath.

- I usually have one or two glasses of water and take supplements. The consistent ones are vitamin D3, omega-3, calcium, and biotin. I have also had a regimen that included Femmenessence Macapause, Cortisol Manager, and Rhodiola tincture (alcohol free).

- If I have a demanding day, I'll throw on clothes as soon as I wake up and take a ten-minute walk to sort of shock me into a heightened alertness before I begin my routine.

- I meditate for twenty minutes either on my yoga mat, chair or in the bath. I do reiki on myself for about ten to fifteen minutes and follow this with a seven-minute energy balancing exercise I was given by Lara Riggio (thelaratouch.com). If I'm living with a client, this routine (minus the reiki) becomes our morning routine together. At the end of my meditation, I usually invoke some version of the Eleventh Step Prayer (which I shorten to "Show me what to do and give me the humility to do it") or set some kind of intention for the day.

- I usually spend the next sixty to ninety minutes working. During this time, I might make a protein smoothie (vegetable or whey protein, frozen fruit, coconut milk, and avocado) or breakfast (oatmeal and fruit or eggs and salad).

- I usually don't schedule meetings before 10 a.m. If I have a client Skype session scheduled for early in the morning, I will wake with enough time to do my morning routine first.

- This is where exercise fits in; sometimes I will hit the gym after my first round at my desk (around 10 or 11 a.m.), other times I will continue working and hit a class that starts between 12 to 2 p.m. If I have any kind of deadline or have to prepare contracts or anything time-consuming, I may take a yoga break using a YouTube "Yoga with Adrienne" video.

—5—
NOT-SO-OBVIOUS RECOVERY PRINCIPLE #2:
ENERGY ENGINEERING

"The world belongs to the energetic."
–RALPH WALDO EMERSON

"Every day, women and men become legends."
—COMMON

As a person in recovery, you live and die by your own steam. Most of the time, if you don't devote at least a little bit to doing those things you didn't in active addiction, *you don't feel better in recovery than you did in active addiction.* The trouble is, it isn't all up to you. On some days—and we know you've had those days—you wake up, and you just don't have the energy or motivation you need to meet the challenges you know are coming. Being in recovery can be exhausting, both physically and mentally—and that's on the good days. Maintaining your focus on those days, amid uncertainty and overwhelm, is no easy task. The good days take energy, enthusiasm, and persistence. The hard days take all that and more.

Someone in recovery with low energy suffers greatly. Motivation is hard to sustain. Focus is often generated artificially by stimulants, such as a recovery drug of choice—caffeine. Maintaining sobriety and serenity *requires an abundance of energy*. There's no way around it. You can have the best track record for sobriety, the best intentions, and the best action plan for the day, but if you don't have the *energy* to take advantage of them, reaching your goals is going to be unnecessarily difficult. If you want to maximize recovery, you need energy—the more the better, and the more *consistent* the better.

- Energy is the fuel that enables you to maintain clarity, focus, and action so that you can generate stellar results, day after day.

- Energy is contagious—it spreads from you to the world around you like a positive virus, creating symptoms of enthusiasm and positive responses everywhere.

- Energy is the foundation of everything, and it is what determines the success we attract.

The question is, *how do you strategically engineer your life so that you maintain a high level of sustainable energy*, which is always available to you, on demand?

When we struggle with energy issues, we might try to compensate with caffeine and other stimulants, and they'll work for a while … until we crash. You may have noticed the same thing. You can lean on stimulants to build up energy for a short while, but then the energy seems to fall off just when you need it the most. Can't you just hear one of those infomercial hosts chime in here: *but, Joe and Anna, there's got to be a better way!*

There is…

If you've been fueling yourself on coffee and pure determination, you haven't even begun to reach the heights of achievement that are possible when you understand how energy works and commit to engineer your life for optimum energy.

Natural Energy Cycles

The first thing to understand about energy is that the goal isn't to be running at full speed all the time. It isn't practical to maintain a constant output. As human beings, we have a natural ebb and flow to our energy levels. Being the happiest, healthiest and most serene person in recovery, it turns out, is the same. Know that you will need to access deeper wells of energy during particularly intense times throughout the year, and allow yourself the time to rest, rejuvenate, and recharge when the intensity lessens.

Just like houseplants need water, our energy reserves need regular replenishing. You can go full tilt for long periods of time, but eventually your mind, body, and spirit will need to be refilled. Think of your life as a container that holds your energy. When you do not properly manage what's in your container, it's like having a hole in the bottom. No matter how much you pour in, you still won't feel fully energized.

Instead of letting yourself get to the point of being overwhelmed, burned out, or stressed out, why not become proactive about your energy levels and have an auto-recharge system in place? This will help you plug the holes in your container and allow you to fill up with the energy you need.

If you have resigned yourself to being tired, cranky, behind on your to-do list, out of shape, and unhappy, we have some great news.

Being continually exhausted is not only unacceptable, *you don't have to settle for it*. There are a few simple ways to get what you need and want—more rest, time to replenish and recharge, and inner peace and happiness. A tall order? Yes. Impossible? Heck, no!

This is about strategically engineering your life for optimum and sustainable physical, mental, and emotional energy. Here are the three principles we try to follow to keep our energy reserves at maximum capacity and on tap for whenever we need them.

1. Eat and Drink for Energy

When it comes to energy engineering, what you eat and drink may play the most critical role of all. If you're like most people, you base your food choices on taste first and the consequences second (if you consider them at all). Yet, what pleases our taste buds in the moment doesn't always give us maximum energy to last throughout the day.

There is nothing wrong with eating foods that taste good, but if you want to be truly healthy and have the energy to perform like a champion, here's the big idea: it is crucial that we make a conscious decision to **place more value on the health and energy consequences of food than we do on the taste**. Why? Because digesting food is one of the most energy-draining processes that the body endures. Need evidence? Just take a second to think about how exhausted you feel after a big meal (see: Thanksgiving dinner). It's no coincidence that a large meal is usually followed by heavy eyes and ultimately a nap. They call it a "food coma" for a reason.

Foods like bread, cooked meats, dairy products, and any foods that have been processed require more energy to digest than they contribute to your body. So, rather than giving you energy, these essentially "dead" foods tend to drain your energy to fuel digestion and leave you in an energy deficit. On the other hand, "living" foods like raw fruits, vegetables, nuts, and seeds typically give you more energy than they require for digestion, thus empowering your body and mind with an energy surplus, which enables you to perform at your best.

Put very simply, everything you put into your body either contributes to or detracts from your health and energy. Drinking water puts a check in the plus column; double fists full of chocolate bars don't. Eating a diet rich with fresh fruits and vegetables equals more plusses. Rolling through the drive-thru to wolf down some fast food? Not so much. We know you know the drill. This isn't rocket science, but it may be the single most important area of your life to optimize. You may need to stop fooling yourself.

If you're not already doing so, it's time to be intentional and strategic about what you eat, when you eat, and—most importantly—*why* you eat so that you can engineer your life for optimum energy.

Strategic Eating

Up until this point, you may have been wondering, *When the heck do I get to eat during my Miracle Morning?* We'll cover that here. We'll also address *what* to eat for maximum energy, which is critical, and *why* what you choose to eat may be most important consideration of all.

When to Eat – Again, remember that digesting food is one of the most energy-draining processes the body goes through each day. The bigger the meal, the more food you give your body to digest, the more drained you will feel. With that in mind, we recommend eating your first meal *after* your Miracle Morning. This ensures that, for optimum alertness and focus during the S.A.V.E.R.S., your blood will be flowing to your brain rather than to your stomach to digest your food.

However, we do recommend starting your day by ingesting a small amount of healthy fats, as fuel for your brain. Studies show that keeping your mind sharp and your moods in balance may be largely related to the type of fat you eat. "Our brain is at least 60 percent fat, and it's composed of fats (like omega-3s) that must be obtained from the diet," says Amy Jamieson-Petonic, MEd, a registered dietitian, the director of wellness coaching at the Cleveland Clinic, and a national spokesperson for the American Dietetic Association.

After drinking his first full glass of water, Hal starts every morning with a tablespoon of organic coconut butter (specifically Nutiva Organic Coconut Manna, which you can order from Amazon.com) and a large mug of organic coffee, which he blends with Bulletproof Cacao Butter (available on Bulletproof.com). The tablespoon of coconut butter is such a small amount that it's easily digested, and it contains healthy fats to provide fuel for the brain. And the health benefits of cacao are significant, from being a powerhouse full of antioxidants (cacao rates in the top 20 on the oxygen radical absorbance capacity, a.k.a. ORAC, scale, which is used to rate the antioxidant capacity of foods) to lowering blood pressure.

Maybe most exciting is that eating cacao actually makes you happy! It contains phenylethylamine (known as the "love drug"), which is responsible for our state of mood and pleasure and delivers the same feelings you get when you are in love. It also acts as a stimulant and can improve mental alertness. In other words, cacao = win, win, win!

If you do feel like you must eat a meal first thing in the morning, make sure that it's a small, light, easily digestible meal, such as fresh fruit or a smoothie (more on that in a minute).

Why to Eat – Let's take a moment to delve deeper into *why* you choose to eat the foods that you do. When you're shopping at the grocery store or selecting food from a menu at a restaurant, what criteria do you use to determine which foods you are going to put into your body? Are your choices based purely on taste? Texture? Convenience? Are they based on health? Energy? Dietary restrictions?

Most people eat the foods they do based mainly on the *taste* and, at a deeper level, based on our emotional attachment to the foods we like the taste of. If you were to ask someone, "Why did you eat that ice cream? Why did you drink that soda?" Or, "Why did you bring that fried chicken home from the grocery store?" You would most likely hear responses like, "Mmm, because I love ice cream! … I like drinking soda. … I was in the mood for fried chicken." All of these answers are based on the emotional enjoyment derived primarily from the way these foods taste. In this case, this person is not likely to explain their food choices by stating how much value these foods will add to their health or how much sustained energy they'll receive as a result of ingesting them.

Our point is this: if we want to have more energy (which we all do) and if we want our lives to be healthy and disease-free (which we all do), then it is crucial that we reexamine why we eat the foods that we do. From this point forward—and we know we've covered this, but it bears repeating—*start placing significantly more value on the health and energy consequences of the foods you eat than you do on the taste.* The taste only provides you with a few minutes of pleasure, but the health and energy consequences impact the rest of your day and, ultimately, the rest of your life.

Again, in no way are we saying that we should eat foods that don't taste good in exchange for the health and energy benefits. We're saying that we can have both. We're saying that if we want to live every day with an abundance of energy so we can perform at our best and live long, healthy lives, we must choose to eat more foods that are good for our health and give us sustained energy, as well as taste great.

What to Eat – Before we talk about what to eat, let's take a second to talk about what to *drink*. Remember that step four of the Five-Step Snooze-Proof Wake-Up Strategy is to drink a full glass of water—first thing in the morning—so you can rehydrate and reenergize after a full night of sleep.

As for what to eat, it has been proven that a diet rich in *living foods*, such as fresh fruits and vegetables, will greatly increase your energy levels, improve your mental focus and emotional well-being, keep you healthy, and protect you from disease. So, Hal created The Miracle Morning Super-Food Smoothie that incorporates everything your body needs in one tall, frosty glass! We're talking about complete protein (*all* of the essential amino acids), age-defying antioxidants, omega-3 essential fatty acids (to boost immunity, cardiovascular health, and brain power), plus a rich spectrum of vitamins and minerals… and that's just for starters. We haven't even mentioned all the *super-foods*, such as the stimulating, mood-lifting phytonutrients in cacao (the tropical bean from which chocolate is made), the long-lasting energy of maca (the Andean adaptogen revered for its hormone-balancing effects), and the immune-boosting nutrients and appetite-suppressing properties of chia seeds.

The Miracle Morning Super-Food Smoothie not only provides you with sustained energy, it also tastes great. You might even find that it enhances your ability to create miracles in your everyday life. You can download and print the recipe for free at www.TMMBook.com.

Remember the old saying *you are what you eat?* Take care of your body so your body will take care of you. You will feel vibrant energy and enhanced clarity immediately!

We have shifted our view of food from that of a reward, treat, or comfort, to that of fuel. We want to eat delicious, healthy foods that boost our energy levels and allow us to keep going as long as we need to go.

Don't get us wrong; we still enjoy certain foods that are not the healthiest choices, but we try to reserve them for times when we don't need to maintain optimum energy levels, such as in the evenings and on weekends.

The easiest way for us to start making better decisions about our eating was to start paying attention to the way we felt after eating certain foods. It doesn't take long for us to recognize which foods give us the biggest power boost and which ones don't.

What would it be like to give your body what it needs to work and play for as long as you like? What would it be like to give yourself exactly what you truly deserve? Give yourself the gift of great health, consciously chosen through what you eat and drink.

If you are eating throughout the day almost as an afterthought, maybe hitting a drive-thru after you've reached the point of being famished, it is time to start building a new strategy.

Give some thought to the following:

- Can I start to consciously consider the consequences (both in health and energy) of what I eat and value that above the taste?

- Can I keep water with me so that I can hydrate with intention and purpose and avoid becoming dehydrated?

- Can I plan my meals in advance, including incorporating healthy snacks, so I can combat any patterns I have that don't serve me?

Yes, you can do all of these, and much more. Think about how much better your life will be and how much more energy you will have for your business and life when you become conscious and intentional about your eating and drinking habits.

- You will easily maintain a positive mental and emotional state. Low energy causes us to feel down, whereas high energy levels produce a positive state of mind, outlook, and attitude.

- You will be more disciplined. Low energy drains our willpower, making us more likely to choose doing the *easy* things over the *right* things. High energy levels increase our level of self-discipline.

- You will live longer.

- You will set an example for the people around you and the people you love. How we live our lives gives permission to those around us to do the same.

- You will get healthier, feel much better, and live longer.

- Bonus—you will settle at your natural weight effortlessly.

- Best Bonus Ever—your recovery will thrive because you'll look and feel great.

Don't forget to stay hydrated throughout the day. Lack of water can lead to dehydration, a condition that occurs when you don't have enough water in your body to carry out normal functions. Even mild dehydration can drain your energy and make you tired.

By implementing the Five-Step Snooze-Proof Wake-Up Strategy, you'll have had your first glass of water at the start of the day. Beyond that, we recommend keeping a large water bottle with you and make a habit of drinking sixteen ounces every one to two hours. If remembering is a challenge for you, set a recurring timer or add multiple alarms on your phone to hold you accountable. Every time you hear a reminder, drink what's left in your water bottle and refill it for the next round of rehydration. Keeping a full bottle with you will allow you to take in water as needed as well.

When it comes to frequency of eating, it's important to refuel every three to four hours, with small, easily digestible, living foods.

In the end, here is the simple thing to remember: food is fuel. We should use it to get us from the beginning of the day all the way to the end, feeling great and having plenty of energy. Placing more value on the energy consequences of the foods you eat above the taste, along with eating foods that fuel energy, is the first step in energy engineering.

2. Sleep and Wake to Win

Sleep more to achieve more. That might be the most counterintuitive productivity mantra you'll ever hear, but it's true. The body needs enough shut-eye each night to function properly and to recharge after a demanding day. Sleep also plays a critical role in immune function, metabolism, memory, learning, and other vital bodily functions. It's when the body does most its repairing, healing, resting, and growing.

If you don't sleep enough, you're gradually wearing yourself down.

Sleeping Versus Sleeping *Enough*

But how much is enough? There is a big difference between the amount of sleep you can get by on and the amount you need to function optimally. Researchers at the University of California, San Francisco discovered that some people have a gene that enables them to do well on six hours of sleep a night. This gene, however, is very rare, appearing in less than 3 percent of the population. For the other 97 percent of us, six hours doesn't come close to cutting it. Just because you're able to function on five to six hours of sleep doesn't mean you wouldn't feel a lot better and get more done if you spent an extra hour or two in bed.

That may sound counterintuitive. We can almost hear you thinking, *Spend more time in bed and get more done? How does that work?* But it has been well-documented that enough sleep allows the body to function at higher levels of performance. You'll not only work better and faster, but your attitude will improve, too.

The amount of nightly rest each individual needs differs, but research shows that the average adult needs approximately seven to eight hours of sleep to restore the energy it takes to handle all of the demands of living each day.

The best way to figure out if you're meeting your sleep needs is to evaluate how you feel as you go about your day. If you're logging enough hours, you'll feel energetic and alert all day long, from the moment you wake up until your regular bedtime. If you're not, you'll reach for caffeine or sugar mid-morning or mid-afternoon … or both.

If you're like most people, when you don't get enough rest you have difficulty concentrating, thinking clearly, and even remembering things. You might notice your ineffectiveness or inefficiencies at home or at work or even blame these missteps on your busy schedule. The more sleep you miss, the more pronounced your symptoms become.

In addition, a lack of rest and relaxation can really work a number on your mood. Recovery is no place for crankiness! It is a scientific fact that when individuals miss out on good nightly rest, their personalities are affected, and they are generally grumpier, less patient, and more apt to snap at people. Missing out on critical, much-needed rest might make you a bear to be around, which is not much fun for anyone, yourself included.

Most adults cut back on their sleep to pack more activities into their day. As you run against the clock to beat deadlines, you might be tempted to skimp on sleep in order to get more done. Unfortunately, lack of sleep can cause the body to run down, which allows illnesses, viruses, and diseases the tiny opening they need to attack the body. When you are sleep deprived, your immune system can become compromised and susceptible to just about anything. Eventually, lack of rest can cause illness that leads to missed days or even weeks of work. That's no way to improve your life.

On the flip side, when you get enough sleep, your body runs as it should, you're pleasant to be around, and your immune system is stronger. And that's precisely when you'll make more sales and attract more people into your business. Think of good sleep as the time when you turn on your inner magnet. Wake up rested and start your day in a great mood because of your S.A.V.E.R.S., and you'll attract more opportunities because a happy person is also a rich one.

The True Benefits of Sleep

You may not realize how powerful sleep truly is. While you're happily wandering through your dreams, sleep is doing some hard work on your behalf and delivering a host of amazing benefits.

Sleep improves your memory. Your mind is surprisingly busy while you snooze. Sleep allows you to clean out damaging toxins that are byproducts of brain function during the day, strengthen memories and practice skills learned while you were awake through a process called consolidation.

"If you are trying to learn something, whether it's physical or mental, you learn it to a certain point with practice," says Dr. David Rapoport, who is an associate professor at NYU Langone Medical Center and a sleep expert, "but something happens while you sleep that makes you learn it better."

In other words, if you're trying to learn something new, whether it's Spanish, a new tennis swing, or the specifications of a new product in your arsenal, you'll perform better when you get adequate sleep.

Sleep can help you live longer. Too much or too little sleep is associated with a shorter life span, although it's not clear if it's a cause or an effect. In a 2010 study of women ages fifty to seventy-nine, more deaths occurred in women who got fewer than five hours or more than six-and-a-half hours of sleep per night. Getting the right amount of sleep is a good idea for your long-term health.

Sleep boosts creativity. Get a good night's sleep before grabbing the easel and paintbrushes or the pen and paper. In addition to consolidating memories or making them stronger, your brain appears to reorganize and restructure them, which may result in more creativity as well.

Researchers at Harvard University and Boston College found that people seem to strengthen the emotional components of a memory during sleep, which may help spur the creative process.

Sleep assists in attaining and maintaining a healthy weight. If you're overweight, you won't have the same energy levels as those at a healthy weight. If you are changing your lifestyle to include more exercise and diet changes, you'll want to plan an earlier bedtime. Putting additional physical demands on your body means you will need to counterbalance those demands with enough rest.

The good news: researchers at the University of Chicago found that dieters who were well-rested lost more fat—up to 56 percent more—than those who were sleep deprived, who lost more muscle mass. Dieters in the study also felt hungrier when they got less sleep. Sleep and metabolism are controlled by the same sectors of the brain, and when you are sleepy, certain hormones—those that drive appetite—go up in your blood.

Sleep lets you feel less stressed. When it comes to our health, stress and sleep are closely connected, and both can affect cardiovascular health. Sleep can reduce stress levels, and with that comes better control of blood pressure. It is also believed that sleep affects cholesterol levels, which play a significant role in heart disease.

Sleep helps you avoid mistakes and accidents. The National Highway Traffic Safety Administration reported in 2009 that being tired accounted for the highest number of fatal, single-car, run-off-the-road crashes due to the driver's performance—even more than alcohol! Sleepiness is grossly underrated as a problem by most people, but the cost to society is enormous. Lack of sleep affects reaction time and decision-making.

If insufficient sleep for only one night can be as detrimental to your driving ability as having an alcoholic drink, imagine how it affects your ability to maintain the focus necessary to become a top entrepreneur or employee.

So, how many hours of sleep do you *really* need? You tell us, because only you truly know how much sleep you need to hit home run after home run. Now, if you really struggle with falling or staying asleep, and it is a concern for you, Shawn Stevenson's book, *Sleep Smarter: 21 Proven Tips to Sleep Your Way to a Better Body, Better Health, and Bigger Success,* is one of the most well-written and thoroughly researched books on the topic of sleep.

Getting consistent and effective rest is as critical to performing at your best as what you do or don't have in your diet. A good night's sleep provides the basis for a day of clear thought, sustained energy, and peak performance. You probably already know how many hours you need to be at your best, and it's important that you are optimizing your sleep. However, what may be even more important than how many hours of sleep you get each night is how you approach the act of waking up in the morning.

You Snooze, You Lose: The Truth About Waking Up

The old saying, "you snooze, you lose" may have a much deeper meaning than any of us realized. When you hit the snooze button and delay waking up until you *have* to—meaning you wait until the time when you have to be somewhere, do something, or take care of someone else—consider that you're starting your day with resistance. Every time you hit the snooze button, you're in a state of resistance to your day, to your life, and to waking up and creating the life you say you want.

According to Robert S. Rosenberg, medical director of the Sleep Disorders Centers of Prescott Valley and Flagstaff, Arizona, "When you hit the snooze button repeatedly, you're doing two negative things to yourself. First, you're fragmenting what little extra sleep you're getting so it is of poor quality. Second, you're starting to put yourself through a new sleep cycle that you aren't giving yourself enough time to finish. This can result in persistent grogginess throughout the day."

If you're not already, make sure you start following the Five-Minute Snooze-Proof Wake-Up Strategy in chapter two, and you'll be poised to win. If getting to bed on time is your challenge, try setting a "bedtime alarm" that sounds an hour before your ideal bedtime, prompting you to start winding down so you can hit the sack.

On the other hand, when you wake up each day with passion and purpose, you join the small percentage of high achievers who are living their dreams. Most importantly, you will be happy. By simply changing your approach to waking up in the morning, you will literally change everything. But don't take our word for it—trust these famous early risers: Oprah Winfrey, Tony Robbins, Bill Gates, Howard Schultz, Deepak Chopra, Wayne Dyer, Thomas Jefferson, Benjamin Franklin, Albert Einstein, Aristotle, and far too many more to list here.

No one ever taught us that by learning how to consciously set our intention to wake up each morning with a genuine desire—even enthusiasm—we can change our entire lives.

If you're just snoozing every day until the last possible moment you have to head off to work, show up for school, or take care of your family, and then coming home and zoning out in front of the television until you go to bed (this used to be Hal's daily routine), we've got to ask you: When are you going to develop yourself into the person you need to be to create the levels of health, happiness, serenity, and freedom that you truly want and deserve? When are you going to actually live your life instead of numbly going through the motions looking for every possible distraction to escape reality? What if your reality—your life—could finally be something that you can't wait to be conscious for?

There is no better day than today for us to give up who we've been for who we can become and to upgrade the life we've been living for the one we really want. There is no better book than the one you are holding in your hands to show you how to become the person you need to be—the one who is capable of quickly attracting, creating and sustaining the life you have always wanted.

How Much Sleep Do We *Really* Need?

The first thing experts will tell you about how many hours of sleep we need is that there is no universal number. The ideal duration of sleep varies from person to person and is influenced by factors such as age, genetics, stress, overall health, how much exercise a person gets, our diet—including how late we eat our last meal—and countless other factors.

For example, if your diet consists of fast food, processed foods, excessive sugar, etc., then your body will be challenged to recharge and rejuvenate while you sleep, as it will be working all night to detoxify and filter out the poisons that you've put into it. On the other hand, if you eat a clean diet made up of living food, as we covered in the last section, then your body will recharge and rejuvenate much more easily. The person who eats a clean diet will almost always wake feeling refreshed, with more energy, and better able to function optimally, even from less sleep, than the person who eats poorly.

According to the National Sleep Foundation, some research has found that long sleep durations (nine hours or more) are also associated with increased morbidity (illness, accidents) and even mortality (death.) This research also found that variables such as depression were significantly associated with long sleep.

Since there is such a wide variety of opposing evidence from countless studies and experts, and since the amount of sleep needed varies from person to person, we're not going to attempt to make a case that there is one right approach to sleep. Instead, we'll share Hal's own real-world results, from personal experience, experimentation, and studying the sleep habits of some of the greatest minds in history. We'll warn you, some of this may be somewhat controversial.

How to Wake Up with More Energy (On Less Sleep)

Through experimenting with various sleep durations—as well as learning those of many other Miracle Morning practitioners who have tested this theory—Hal found that how our sleep affects our biology is largely impacted by our own personal *belief* about how much sleep we need. In other words, how we feel when we wake up in the morning— and this is a very important distinction—is not solely based on how many hours of sleep we got but rather significantly impacted by how we *told* ourselves we were going to feel when we woke up.

For example, if you *believe* that you need eight hours of sleep to feel rested, but you're getting into bed at midnight and have to wake up at 6:00 a.m., you're likely to tell yourself, "Geez, I'm only going to get six hours of sleep tonight, but I need eight. I'm going to feel exhausted in the morning." Then, what happens as soon as your alarm clock goes off and you realize it's time to wake up? What's your first thought? It's the same thought you had before bed! "Geez, I only got six hours of sleep. I feel exhausted." It's a self-fulfilling, self-sabotaging prophecy. If you tell yourself you're going to feel tired in the morning, then you are absolutely going to feel tired. If you believe that you need eight hours to feel rested, then you're not going to feel rested on anything less. But what if you changed your beliefs?

The mind-body connection is a powerful thing, and we believe we must take responsibility for every aspect of our lives, including the power to wake up every day feeling energized, regardless of how many hours of sleep we get.

So, how many hours of sleep do you *really* need? You tell us.

3. Rest to Recharge

The conscious counterpart to sleep is *rest*. While some people use the terms interchangeably, they're quite different. You might get eight hours of sleep, but if you spend all of your waking hours on the go, then you won't have any time to think or recharge your physical, mental, and emotional batteries. When you work all day, run from activity to activity after hours, and then finish with a quick dinner and a late bedtime, you don't allow for a period of rest.

Likewise, spending weekends taking the kids to soccer, volleyball, or basketball, then heading out to see a football game, going to meetings, singing in the choir, attending several birthday parties, etc., can do more harm than good. While each of these activities is great individually, maintaining a fully-packed schedule doesn't allow for time to recharge.

We live in a culture that perpetuates the belief that when our days are busy and exciting, we are more valuable, more important, or more alive. In truth, we are all of those things when we can be at peace within our own skin. Despite our best intentions to live balanced lives, the modern world demands that we are almost always connected and productive, and these demands can drain us emotionally, spiritually, and physically.

What if, instead of being constantly on the go, you valued intentional quiet time, sacred space, and periods of purposeful silence? How might that improve your life, your physical and emotional well-being, and your ability to achieve success in recovery?

It may seem counterintuitive to take time out when your to-do list is a mile long, but the fact is that more rest is a pre-requisite to truly productive work.

Research proves that rest melts your stress away. Practices like yoga and meditation also lower heart rates, blood pressure, and oxygen consumption, as well as alleviating hypertension, arthritis, insomnia, depression, infertility, cancer, and anxiety. The spiritual benefits of resting are profound. Slowing down and getting quiet means you can actually hear your own wisdom, your inner knowledge, and your inner voice. Rest and its close sibling, relaxation, allow us to reconnect with the world around us, inviting ease and a sense of contentment into our lives.

And yes, in case you're wondering, you'll be more productive, nicer to your friends and family members (not to mention your fellow employees), and in general much happier as well. When we rest, it's like letting the earth lie fallow rather than constantly planting and harvesting. Our personal batteries need to be recharged. The best way to recharge them is to truly and simply rest.

Easy Ways to Rest

Most of us confuse rest with recreation. To rest, we do things like hike, garden, work out, or even party. Any of these activities can only be termed restful because they are breaks from work, but truthfully, they are not, and cannot be, defined as rest.

Rest has been defined as a kind of waking sleep, experienced while you are alert and aware. Rest is the essential bridge to sleep, and we achieve rest and sleep the same way: by making space for them and allowing them to happen. Every living organism needs rest, including you. When we don't take the time to rest, eventually its absence takes a toll on the body.

If you are now investing five or more minutes each morning, during your S.A.V.E.R.S., to meditate or sit in silence, that is a great start.

- You can reserve Sundays or, if Sunday is a busy workday for you, choose another day of the week for rest. You can read, watch a movie, or do something else low-key. Maybe try cooking a delicious meal.

- When you're driving, drive in silence: turn off the radio and stow your phone.

- Go for a walk without your earbuds in. Even a walk in nature without intention or goals, such as burning calories, can work.

- Turn off the television. Designate a half hour, an hour, or even half a day for silence. Try taking a few conscious breaths, during which you focus on your inhale and exhale or the space between breaths.

- You can also mindfully drink a cup of tea, read something inspirational, write in your journal, take a hot bath, or get a massage.

- Attend a retreat. It could be with a group of friends, your family, other friends in recovery or spending time on your own in nature.

It's helpful to set a specific time for rest. Put boundaries around it so you can claim that time.

The Rest Habit

As someone in recovery, you're in the trenches by default. You'll need to schedule your time for rest and self-care in the same way you schedule the other appointments in your life. The energy you get back will reward you many times over.

Rest certainly isn't something we were taught in school, and it may not come naturally at first. So, you may find that you need to consciously make it a priority. Learning different mindfulness practices and bringing them into your everyday life is an effective way to deeply rest your body, mind, and spirit. These practices—such as mid-day meditation, yoga, and purposeful silence—are powerful ways to go within and achieve restful states of being, particularly when you commit to practicing them regularly.

The more you integrate periods of rest and silence into your daily life, the bigger the payoff will be. During more tranquil periods, perhaps you won't need to rest as much, but periods of intensity (such as meeting a huge quota or a big deadline) may require more rest and silence than usual.

Combining exercise, healthy food choices, consistent sleep, and rest will give you a quantum leap in the right direction for you and your business or career. Keep in mind that when you try to adopt these three practices—to eat, sleep, and rest more effectively—you may at first find them to be uncomfortable. Your mind and body may encounter some emotional resistance. Resist the urge to run from the discomfort by making a commitment to begin putting them into practice, today.

Putting Energy Engineering into Action

Step One: Commit to eating and drinking for energy by prioritizing the energy consequences of the foods you eat above the taste. After your initial glass of water in the morning, ingest some form of healthy fat to fuel your brain. Try incorporating one new healthy meal, made up of *living* foods, into your diet each day. Instead of snacking on potato chips, try kale chips or fresh organic fruit. And remember to keep a full bottle of water with you all the time to stay hydrated.

Step Two: Sleep and wake to win by choosing a consistent daily bedtime *and* wake-up time. Based on what time you wake up to do your Miracle Morning, back your way into a bedtime that ensures you will get enough sleep. Maintain a specific bedtime for a few weeks to get your body acclimated. If you need a little nudge to get to bed on time, set a bedtime alarm that prompts you to start winding down one hour before bedtime. After a couple of weeks, feel free to play with the number of hours you leave for sleeping to optimize your energy levels.

Step Three: Incorporate time into your daily calendar to rest and recharge, whether that's meditation, a nap, going for a walk, or doing an activity that brings you joy. Remember, Hal takes a two-hour lunch break every day, which gives him time to either play basketball or wakeboard—two activities that he loves to do and that thoroughly reenergize him. Which activities can you plan into your day that will reenergize you? In addition to your Miracle Morning routine, schedule regular daily periods to rest and recharge.

Now that you have a plan for your body, let's direct our attention to focus.

RECOVERY WARRIOR MORNING ROUTINE

WES GEER

FACEBOOK.COM/ROCKTORECOVERY

TWITTER/INSTAGRAM: @WESGEER

Wesley Geer is a professional guitar player, songwriter, recording artist, and producer who signed his first record deal to Jive Records with the band he founded, (Hed) P.E. Wes toured the world for nearly a decade, and the band sold over one million records worldwide. Their music was on high rotation on MTV and radio stations, as well as having numerous placements in popular feature films, TV and video games. In 2010, Geer was offered the gig as guitarist with the legendary rock band Korn. He traveled the world, performing in more than forty countries with the multi-platinum stars, as well as appearing in numerous live televised and studio recording sessions. In 2012, he founded Rock to Recovery (R2R), a non-profit organization with the purpose of providing those in various types of treatment and recovery programs the cathartic, uplifting, healing experience of connectivity through playing music. Rock to Recovery, including Geer and his staff of nine fellow sober musicians, now partners with over 100 treatment programs across LA, Orange and San Diego counties, providing more than 400 sessions each month to people struggling with addiction, mental health, and eating disorders, as well as at–risk youth and Wounded Warriors.

Wes's morning routine:

- I'm usually up around 6:30 a.m., and the first thing I do is get up and make my bed.

- Next, I think briefly about my day, where I am at mentally/ emotionally/physically. Maybe I need focus and direction, or guidance on a project. Maybe I need release of worry and stress. I take this information into my prayers. I get on my knees, elbows on my bed, hands clasped, and I start praying.

- The first thing I say is, "God, thank you for this day, this life, my health," and a few other things that come to mind—a recent hang with friends, an interaction with Mom. I name a few specific things I am thankful for, and then I move to asking for help for what I need specifically (as designated from above). I never tell God or the Universe what to do, rather, I ask for guidance in doing it best/well/properly.

- If I need to—when my self-esteem is low, when I feel beat up by life—I follow with some affirmations. I use "I am" statements when doing this.

- Sometimes in this prayer session, I will say, "It is now my intention to bring forth the perfect _____." I got this from the book *I Am the Word*. I'm not asking for the specific result, but the perfect version God/the Universe decides for me.

- The prayers above take just a minute usually.

- Next, it's time to coffee up. I put on organic coffee, using the French Press. No cream. No sugar. I clean the kitchen up while I'm waiting. It makes me feel good, helps me come to. I'll just kick it for ten to fifteen minutes, just drinking coffee, not doing much yet.

- I also light candles. I burn Palo Santo, which for some reason instantly makes me feel more connected to the spirit world.

- Once the coffee is done, I start drinking it, of course, and get whatever spiritual text I am reading ready. I read a couple pages, and when I get some stuff that really resonates and gets me thinking on what I need to work on spiritually or that I need to manifest, I meditate on that. It could be I just need serenity. It could be feeling lack/scarcity in my life, so I'll meditate on the infinite abundance of the Universe. Oftentimes I need answers, guidance, and I bring those questions into meditation and just listen. It's amazing how fast I "hear" answers, from a Source I know is not me, saying things I never thought of...I actually was meditating and ended up talking to a deceased friend once. Who knew if we were connected or not? But I asked, "Hey, is there anything you want me to do down here?" Why I asked that, I'll never know. Instantly, and it usually happens this way, this (his) voice said, before I even finished asking the question, "YES. Get ahold of my mother." I never met this guy's mother in my life! Within five minutes of my meditation, she called me, saying her (deceased) son told her to get ahold of me as well.

- I may or may not listen to some cool meditation music while I'm going deep.

- Prior to starting meditation, I get my organic, gluten-free, steel-cut oatmeal going; it cooks in the perfect time to read and do a twenty-minute meditation.

- Meditation is HUGE for me...asking for guidance and direction, giving me peace when I'm freaking out. So many ways I use it. So many benefits. One is just separating thoughts from *me*. I am NOT my thoughts. This helps me to be able to observe them, and not BE them. I am the observer of my thoughts.

- After that, it's time to eat. I use vanilla almond milk, some organic granola, and a ton of fresh organic blueberries, strawberries, and bananas on the cereal.

- I change and get ready for the gym.

- I write up my list of things to do that day, helped by meditating, listening, praying.

- Off to the gym by 8 a.m.

- I work out for an hour, running for about fifteen minutes, then a light cycle through a few stretches and lifting.

- Then it's time to get home, shower (maybe LOL), and get to work!

NOT-SO-OBVIOUS RECOVERY PRINCIPLE #3:

UNWAVERING FOCUS

"You need to get up, get out and get something.
Don't let the days of your life pass by."
—OUTKAST FT. GOODIE MOBB

We've all met that person. You know—*that* person. The one who runs marathons, coaches little league, volunteers at her son's school lunch program, and maybe writes a novel on the side. And on top of all that? She's a role model in recovery, getting tons of accolades, and knocking it out of the park year after year. We bet you know someone like that—someone who just seems inexplicably productive.

Or maybe you know *this* person—the person in recovery who also has a wonderful personal and professional life, but never seems to be working on it. He's always playing golf, or out on the lake, in the middle of the workweek. Every time you see him, he's either talking about the vacation he just got back from or the one he's getting ready to leave for. He's fit, always happy, and makes every person he encounters feel like a million bucks.

What you might not realize, though, is exactly how they do it. Maybe you always thought they were lucky. Or gifted. Or connected. Or had the right personality. Or were born with superpowers!

While those things can help when it comes to recovery, we know from experience that the real superpower behind every unbelievably productive person is *unwavering focus.* Unwavering focus is the ability to maintain clarity about your highest priorities and to take all the energy you've learned to generate for yourself, channel it into what matters most, and keep it there, regardless of what is going on around you or how you feel. This ability is key to becoming an exceptional performer.

When you harness the power of focus, you don't become superhuman, but you can achieve seemingly superhuman results. And the reasons for this are surprisingly straightforward.

- **Unwavering focus makes you more effective.** Being effective doesn't mean doing the most things or doing things the fastest. It means doing the *right* things. You engage in the activities that create forward momentum toward your life's goals.

- **Unwavering focus makes you more efficient.** Being efficient means doing things with the fewest resources, such as time, energy, or money. Every time your mind wanders away from your goals, you waste those things—particularly time. In pursuit of our goals, time is always in demand, so every moment that your focus wavers is another moment lost.

- **Unwavering focus makes you more productive**. Understand that just because you're *busy* does not mean you're productive. Too often we confuse being busy—which typically involves engaging in activities that don't produce results, like checking emails or cleaning your car or reorganizing your to-do list for the twelfth time this month—with being productive. When you have a clear vision, identify your highest priorities, and consistently execute your most leveraged activities, you'll go from being busy to being productive. By taking the steps that we're about to cover, you'll learn how to develop the habit of unwavering focus and join the ranks of the most productive people in the world.

If you combine those benefits, you will achieve *a lot* more. Perhaps the greatest value of focus, however, is that rather than scattering your energy across multiple areas of your life and getting mediocre results across the board, you will release untapped potential *and* improve your life.

Now, let's turn your Miracle Morning to the task. Here are four steps that will help you to follow your Miracle Morning with sustained focus.

1. Find Your Best Environment(s) for Unwavering Focus.

Let's start here: *you need an environment that supports your commitment to unwavering focus*. It might be your spare bedroom, or it could be your backyard. No matter how modest, though, you need a place where you go to focus.

Part of the reason for this is simple logistics. If your materials are scattered from the trunk of your car to the kitchen counter, you can't be effective. A bigger reason, however, is that **having a place where you focus triggers the habit of focusing**. Sit at the same desk at the same time every day, and soon enough you'll find yourself slipping into the zone to do great work just by sitting down in that chair.

If you travel a lot, then your car, your suitcase, your hotel rooms, and possibly random coffee shops are part of your focus space too. Build habits for how you pack and work on the road, and you can trigger great focus the same way you do at the office. When you are prepared and always have with you exactly what you need, you can work anywhere.

2. Clear the Unfocused Clutter

Clutter is a focus killer, so clearing it is our next stop on the journey. There is a reason that Marie Kondo's book, *The Life-Changing*

Magic of Tidying Up, is one of the best-selling non-fiction books of the last decade; decluttering both your physical and mental space will inspire a calm, motivated mindset.

There are two kinds of clutter, mental and physical, and we all have them both. We carry around thoughts in our minds, like these: *My sister's birthday is coming up. I should get her a gift and card. I had a great time at dinner the other night. I need to send the host a thank-you note. I must answer the email from my new client before I leave the office today.*

Then there are the physical items we accumulate: stacks of paper, old magazines, sticky notes, clothes we never wear, the pile of junk in the garage. Not to mention the trinkets, knick-knacks, and tokens that accumulate as we go through life.

Clutter of either type creates the equivalent of a heavy fog, and to become focused, you need to be able to *see.* To clear your vision, you'll want to get those mental items out of your head and collected elsewhere so you can relieve the mental stress of trying to remember them. And then, you'll want to get those physical items out of your way.

Here's a simple process to help you clear the fog and create the clarity you need to focus.

- **Create a master to-do list**. You probably have lots of things you haven't written down yet—start with those. Add the contents of all those sticky notes that clutter your desk, computer screen, planner, countertops, and refrigerator (are there other places?). Put those notes and action items on your master list in one central location, whether that's a physical journal or a list on your phone, so that you can clear your mental storage. Feeling better? Keep going; we're just getting started.

- **Purge your workspace.** Schedule a half (or full) day to go through every stack of paper, file folder stuffed with documents, and tray full of unopened mail—you get the gist. Throw out or shred what you don't need. Scan or file the ones that matter. Note in your journal any items that need your attention and cannot be delegated, then pick a time in your schedule to complete them.

- **Declutter your life.** Clean up and clear out every possible drawer, closet, cabinet, or other space that doesn't give you a sense of calm and peace when you see it. This includes your car interior and trunk. This might take a few hours or a few days. Schedule a short time each day until everything is complete. Saying, "I just need a weekend to declutter," is a sure way to never start. Pick a single drawer and start there. You'll be surprised at how the little bursts of work accumulate. Try S.J. Scott and Barrie Davenport's book, *10-Minute Declutter: The Stress-Free Habit for Simplifying Your Home* for suggestions.

Getting physically and mentally organized will allow you to focus at a level you would never believe possible. It leaves your energy nowhere to go except to what *matters*.

3: Protect Yourself from Interruptions

In addition to writing this book, we both do more work projects than we like to even recall. As you can imagine, our time is critically important to us, just as we're sure yours is to you. We've done different things to try to stay focused—from going places without Wi-Fi to taking social media apps off our phone. Hal's phone, meanwhile, is almost always set on Do Not Disturb mode, which blocks all incoming calls, texts, or notifications like email and social media updates. This is a simple thing that dramatically increases his daily productivity and ability to remain focused on the task at hand. He recommends returning phone calls and emails at pre-designated times, according to your schedule, not everybody else's.

You can apply the same philosophy and strategies to any notifications and/or alerts, social media distractions, as well as your availability for colleagues, friends and family members. Do Not Disturb isn't just a setting on your phone. Let people know when you're available, and when they need to leave you undisturbed.

4. Build a Foundation for Unwavering Focus

Once you identify your focus place and begin the process of decluttering your life, you should experience a remarkable increase in focus simply from clearing the fog in your mind.

Now, it's time to take things to the next level. Hal uses three questions to improve his focus:

- What's working that I should *keep doing* (or do more of)?

- What do I need to *start doing* to accelerate results?

- What do I need to *stop doing* immediately that's holding me back from going to the next level?

If you can answer those three questions and act on the answers, you'll discover a whole new level of productivity you probably didn't think was possible. Let's look at each question in detail.

What Do You Need to *Keep Doing* (or Do More of)?

Let's face it, not all tactics and strategies are created equal. Some work better than others. Some work for a while and then become less effective. Some even make things worse.

Right now, you're probably doing a lot of the right activities, and you'll be nodding right along as you read the coming chapters on embracing your community, cleaning up your body, clearing your mind and blowing up your career. If you already know the things you're doing that are working, jot those down. Perhaps you're already using the Do Not Disturb function, or you're already well into a fitness challenge and feeling stronger each day, for example. Put those on the "what's working" list.

Make sure you're choosing things that contribute to increasing your success as a whole. It's easy to keep the things you *like* doing, but you need to make sure that the activities you're doing are directly related to becoming more successful. Consider the 80/20 rule (originally the Pareto principle), which shows that roughly 80 percent of our results come from 20 percent of our efforts. Which 20 percent of your activities impact 80 percent of your results? It's easy to keep the things that you *like* doing, but this is reality—you need to make sure that the activities you're doing are directly related to the business at hand, as well as putting money in your bank account.

At the end of this chapter, you'll have an opportunity to capture in your journal the activities that are working. (Among them, we hope, will be that you've started doing the Life S.A.V.E.R.S.) Everything that's on that list is a *keep doing* until it's replaced by something even more effective.

For each of the "keep doing" activities on your list, make sure you're completely honest with yourself about *what you need to be doing more of* (in other words, what you're currently not doing enough of). If it's something you think you should be doing, such as training for a marathon or starting a band, but it's not moving you forward toward your important goals, it doesn't belong on your list. Perfection is not one of the goals here. Overworking yourself is ultimately unproductive and takes your focus off the important things.

Keep doing what's working and, depending on how much more you want to achieve, simply do *more* of what's working.

What Do You Need to *Start* Doing?

Once you've captured what's working and determined what you need to do more of, it's time to decide what else you can do to accelerate your success.

We have a few top-shelf suggestions to prime the pump and get you started:

- Get together with friends who are either in recovery or focused on healthy living.

- Clean up every day.

- Every few months, mark up a white board with recovery, personal or professional goals for the next few months.

- Volunteer, either with friends or on your own, ideally in a place where you can help those seeking recovery from addiction.

- Come up with a cause to give your life meaning and focus.

- Learn healthy recipes and cook your meals for the week so that you don't find yourself grabbing something unhealthy (or snatching up all the fries at the diner after recovery meetings).

- Create your *foundational schedule*—that recurring, ideal weekly schedule with a time-blocked calendar—so that every day when you wake up, your highest priorities are already predetermined and planned. Then, make any necessary adjustments on Sunday night for the following week.

Now, we have something to say before you throw up your hands, toss this book across the room or shriek, "Who are they kidding?" We beg of you: do not become overwhelmed here. Keep in mind that Rome, not to mention every other city, wasn't built in a day. You don't need to identify fifty-eight action items and implement them by tomorrow. The great thing about having a daily scribing practice as part of your Miracle Morning means you can capture everything. Then, one or two at a time, add them to your success toolbox until they become habits. Incremental improvements have a magical way of accumulating (much like how staying sober one day at a time, every day in row, eventually means long-term sobriety).

What Do You Need to *Stop* Doing?

By now, you've most likely added a few items to start doing. If you're wondering where the time for these new activities is going to come from, this might be your favorite step of all. It's time to let go of the things you've been doing that don't serve you to make room for the ones that do.

We're fairly sure you do a number of daily activities you will be relieved to stop doing, thankful to delegate to someone else or grateful to release altogether.

Why not stop:

- Eating unhealthy, energy-draining foods that suck the life and motivation out of you?

- Doing unnecessary household chores?
- Replying to texts and emails instantly?
- Answering the phone? (Either let it go to voicemail and reply when the timing works best for you or adopt Joe's signature move—which he eventually got Anna to embrace: record and text audio messages in lieu of calling or texting people. It essentially means you get to leave a voicemail without having to let the phone ring or play phone tag and allows you to pack a lot more in than a regular old text does.)
- Reading and posting on social media sites?
- Watching hours of television every day?
- Beating yourself up or worrying about what you can't change?

Or, if you want to improve your focus dramatically in one simple step, try this easy fix: *stop responding to phone buzzes like a trained seal.*

Do you really need to be alerted when you receive texts, emails, and social media notifications? Nope, didn't think so. Go into the settings of your phone, tablet, and computer and turn all your notifications OFF.

Technology exists for your benefit, and you can take control of it this very minute. How often you check your phone messages, texts, and email can and should be decided by *you*. Let's face it, most of us do not have jobs that will result in a life-or-death situation if we do not respond immediately to a call, text, or email. We don't need to be accessible 24/7/365 except to our significant others and our children. An effective alternative is to schedule times during the day to check on what's happening and determine what needs your immediate attention, what items can be added to your schedule or master to-do list and what can be deleted, ignored, or forgotten.

Final Thoughts on Unwavering Focus

Focus is like a muscle that you build over time. And, like a muscle, you need to show up and do the work to make it grow. Cut yourself some slack if you falter, but keep pushing forward. It will get easier. It might take you time to learn to focus, but every day that you try, you'll continue to get better at it. Ultimately, this is about *becoming* someone who focuses, which starts with seeing yourself as such. We recommend that you add a few lines to your affirmations about your commitment to unwavering focus and what you will do each day to develop it.

Most people would be shocked to discover just how little time they spend on truly important, relevant activities each day. Today, or in the next twenty-four hours, schedule sixty minutes to focus on the *single most important task you do*, and you'll be amazed not only by your productivity but also by how empowering it feels.

By now, you've added some pretty incredible action items and focus areas to your success arsenal. After you complete the steps below, head into the next section, where we will sharpen your recovery skills and combine them with the Life S.A.V.E.R.S. in ways you might not have heard or thought of before! Remember the steps we discussed in this chapter on the importance of unwavering focus and the ways to increase it in your life.

Putting Unwavering Focus into Action

Step One: Choose or create your ideal environment to support unwavering focus. If your focus is optimum when you're working in a public place, such as a coffee shop, schedule focused time-blocks at Starbucks. If you work from home, make sure you've implemented step two, below.

Step Two: Clear your physical and mental clutter. Start by scheduling a half day to clean up your workspace. Then, clear your mind with a brain dump. Unload all those little to-do lists floating around in your head. Create a master to-do list, either on your computer, in your phone, or in your journal.

Step Three: Protect yourself from interruptions, both from yourself—by turning off notifications—and from others, by putting your phone into Do Not Disturb mode and letting your circle of influence know to leave you alone during your focused time-blocks.

Step Four: Start building your unwavering focus lists. Pull out your journal, or open a note on your phone or computer, and create the following three lists:

- **What I need to keep doing (or do more of)**
- **What I need to start doing**
- **What I need to stop doing**

Begin jotting down everything that comes to mind. Review your lists, and determine which activities can be automated, outsourced, or delegated. How much time do you spend on your recovery and other activities that contribute to your overall well-being? Repeat this process until you are clear on what your process is, and start time-blocking your days so that you're spending close to 80 percent of your time on tasks that produce results. Delegate the rest.

You've now got a great handle on how to incorporate the Life S.A.V.E.R.S. into your work and personal life. It's time to go deeper on the topic of recovery. When you're ready, let's begin.

RECOVERY WARRIOR MORNING ROUTINE

TOMMY ROSEN

FACEBOOK.COM/TOMMYROSENOFFICIAL
TWITTER/INSTAGRAM: @TOMMYROSEN

Tommy Rosen is a yoga teacher and addiction recovery expert who has spent the last two decades immersed in recovery and wellness. He holds advanced certifications in both Kundalini and Hatha Yoga and has twenty-six years of continuous recovery from drug addiction

Tommy is the founder of the Recovery 2.0 Global Membership Community, the Recovery 2.0 Online Conference series and the Recovery 2.0 Group Coaching Program. He leads Recovery 2.0 retreats and workshops internationally and presents regularly at yoga conferences and festivals.

Tommy's first book, *Recovery 2.0: Move Beyond Addiction and Upgrade Your Life*, was published by Hay House in 2014.

Tommy and his wife, yoga teacher Kia Miller, travel the world and teach internationally throughout the year.

Tommy's morning routine:

- Sadhana: a daily spiritual practice for physical, mental and emotional well-being.

  The morning Sadhana practice is designed to be a gift of the highest magnitude to oneself. It leads ultimately to a deeper connection with one's highest self and/or the Great Spirit, Higher Power, God or whatever your conception is for the force that underlies all creation.

  While the specific routine I do changes and shifts according to my needs, the elements of my personal Sadhana practice are consistent: yoga, breathwork, chanting and meditation.

- I wake up and take a shower. I dress for practice. I get onto the mat and begin to warm up my spine with simple movements.

I may decide to do a specific yoga set and meditation for forty days, which is about the time it takes to fully realize its benefits.

- I do some pranayama (breath control) exercises and then prepare myself to meditate.

- Sometimes I will chant a mantra. This is not a weird thing to do, but it must be said that I never imagined I would be chanting anything. Then, I realized its power. Chanting positive mantras or affirmations cuts through the ego chatter of the mind, which is generally negative nonsense. It has proven to be one of my most powerful tools for realizing freedom from addiction each day.

- Then, finally, I will meditate, dropping down into silent communion with the conscious aspect of me. There is the mind and its thinking and then there is consciousness and its witnessing.

- Meditation is an opportunity to detach from my thinking and connect with my consciousness.

- Sadhana makes my body feel great and strong. It creates a certain flow of energy that I can feel. My mind calms, and I feel emotionally centered.

- The whole process lasts about one hour, though sometimes it is shorter and sometimes I even miss the practice altogether. On those days, I'm a little less sure, a little less clear and a little more prone to thinking...not my preference.

SECTION III:

YOUR COMMUNITY, BODY, MIND, AND CAREER

— 7 —

LEVEL 10 RECOVERY SKILL #1:

EMBRACE YOUR COMMUNITY

"The haters just bringing me and my people closer, actually."
—DRAKE

When it comes to finding recovery, opinions vary greatly. This is a gentle way of saying that you don't want to be around when a 12-stepper gets into it with someone who believes that Alcoholics Anonymous is a dangerous, antiquated institution that destroys lives. Here's what we've learned about it over the years: no one's right and everyone's right.

There are people who believe ninety days of rehab is essential and those who think you can meditate, chant or hypnotize yourself into sobriety. Some quit drugs but keep drinking; others quit drinking but do drugs. There are many "dry drunks"—those who quit drinking but have not addressed the repressed emotions and pain that started them drinking in the first place—that have a slew of behavior addictions. There are people who substitute heroin for pot, those who get sober through non-spiritual programs like SMART Recovery or ultra-spiritual programs like Celebrate Recovery, as well as folks who do Eye Movement Desensitization and Reprocessing (EMDR), Cognitive Behavioral Therapy (CBT), Dialectical Behavioral Therapy (DBT), many other therapeutic programs that don't involve acronyms, and everything in between.

The one bit of common ground that can be found among all these disparate groups is that most agree that community is crucial for a happy and healthy recovery. You won't find many out there arguing that being around other people who are trying to improve their lives is *bad* for someone's recovery. Whether you're entering a 12-step meeting, group therapy, church group or cult (hey, to each his own), you're bound to be comforted by the fact that you're surrounded by like-minded people probably struggling with the same issues that you are.

SECTION 1

The World's Best Park

The great impact community has on addiction and recovery is actually a proven fact. In the late '70s, a Canadian psychologist named Bruce K. Alexander decided to test his hypothesis that addiction is caused by environment and a lack of community—as opposed to the availability of drugs. For his experiment, he built an enormous rat colony that was 200 times the size of a typical cage. He gave those lucky rats everything a young (or old) rat could dream of: yummy food, balls to play with, tin cans, wood chips, platforms and running wheels galore. But the best treat of all? They got plenty of exposure to members of the opposite sex, not to mention places where they could get down (that is, *mate*). In this Rat Park of every rat's dreams, Alexander placed two dispensers—one that contained morphine and another that was straight-up H20. With those rats happily ensconced in Rat Heaven, he set about placing some less-lucky rats alone in individual cages with access to the same amount of morphine and water, but the only interaction they ever got was with the people who brought them food and water. They couldn't exercise, play or—well, forget mating…they couldn't so much as have a brief catch-up with a pal.

Here's what happened: the rats who were living in isolation got hooked on morphine while those who were luxuriating in Rat Park sampled the morphine only occasionally. In one experiment, the individually caged rats in fact drank *nineteen times more morphine* than the park dwellers. Take that in, please. Then fantasize about what your personal version of Rat Park might include, because that's pretty fun. (On our list: Wi-Fi, chocolate, peanut butter and hammocks, to start.)

In another experiment, Alexander offered those sad, solitary caged rats only morphine to drink. After fifty-seven days, they were then transferred to Rat Park, where there was both morphine and water on tap. One might think, since they'd been getting high for almost two months, those rats would stay on drugs. But they didn't. While they did show original signs of dependence, they eventually opted to forgo the morphine for the water.

Now, this doesn't mean that if you place an active addict in a luxurious spa, replete with delicious food and hourly massages, that person will suddenly become drug-free. But it does suggest that environment matters—a lot. And it means that having a community is crucial.

As Alexander wrote, "Solitary confinement drives people crazy; if prisoners in solitary have the chance to take mind-numbing drugs, they do."

Of course, recovery doesn't end when we put the plug in the jug. This means that a positive social environment isn't only important when getting off drugs or alcohol. It's just as important—if not even more important—once we're in recovery.

Is Everything We Know About Addiction Actually Wrong?

In 2015, a British journalist named Johann Hari hammered home the significance of community with his TED Talk, "Everything You Think You Know About Addiction Is Wrong."

Although his beliefs—that punishing addicts only worsens addiction—weren't new, no one had ever articulated them so well. The talk focused not only on Bruce Alexander's work but also on the "human" version of it—that is, the Vietnam War, where 20 percent of troops were using heroin and 95 percent of them quit afterwards. As Hari put it, humans have "an innate need to bond" and if they don't have other humans around to bond with, they will latch onto whatever's there. As Hari put it, "The opposite of addiction isn't sobriety; it's connection."

SECTION 2

It's not hyperbole to say that Joe's entire life is built around having a community. As the creator of the world's highest-level marketing group, Genius Network, Joe gathers the world's top entrepreneurs, best-selling authors, and industry innovators (including Hal!) for regular meetings. These occasions have not only featured talks by people like Richard Branson, Tony Robbins, Dr. Gabor Mate, John Mackey, Brendon Burchard, Neil deGrasse Tyson, Ariana Huffington, Peter Diamandis, Dan Sullivan, Randi Zuckerberg, JP Sears, Tim Ferriss, John Hagelin, and Steve Forbes, but also provide one of the greatest opportunities for high-level business people to commune.

Jos is currently building Genius Recovery, a community that will do for people in recovery what Genius Network does for entrepreneurs. Made up of a blog, podcast, resources and more, Genius Recovery is connected to Joe's other recovery project, Artists for Addicts. The philosophy behind Artists for Addicts is to use art as a "force for good" to not only help people who have developed addiction problems but also to increase understanding about what addiction actually is, where it comes from and how to truly heal it. Artists for Addict's first project is Black Star, a painting created by Artists for Addicts co-founder Jon Butcher as a tribute to famous people lost to addiction. (If you're interested in purchasing a print of Black Star, go to https://artistsforaddicts.com/.)

Dancing and Singing, Oh My!

For Anna, entering rehab and then 12-step rooms revolutionized her life. She had spent the previous few years holed up in her apartment, with only cats and cocaine for company, and to suddenly be among the living was a revelation in itself. The fact that those people were talking about feelings she'd had but hadn't known how to articulate, and that they were sharing them in intelligent and occasionally amusing ways, opened her up to connecting with other people in a way she never had. Suddenly, she wasn't picking her friends based on how willing they were to drive across the border to Mexico to buy sheets of Xanax at a willing Mexican *farmacia*, but by whether or not they were honest and funny and interested in looking at themselves and growing. Anna had gotten so isolated in her addiction that being easily granted a group of people made facing all the other changes she had to deal with in early sobriety far less terrifying.

While her friends have changed over the years—her "picker" was a bit broken after years of active addiction, so she originally found herself drawn to some less-than-healthy people—maintaining a community has continued to be one of her priorities. After years of isolation during her active addiction, she was actually shocked to discover that she's a people person. While she relishes time alone, it was in early sobriety that she realized she loved and in fact needed to be around people to stay mentally healthy.

Because she was living in a New York studio apartment for several years when she was writing books, making sure she was part of a community required extra effort. This meant, when she was writing her memoir, *Falling for Me*, going to coffee shops where she could be around people even if she wasn't talking to them. This is also when she implemented "Project Study Hall," which is what she called it when she got together with friends to sit together working side-by-side—taking, of course, regular breaks to chat.

Today, she works out of a shared office space. She also does workouts that involve group bonding (hip hop dance class with a group of people that hang out together outside of class). And although she's inarguably tone deaf—and there are terrifying Instagram videos out there to prove it—she plans karaoke nights; when she was the editor of a website and had a team under her, she actually called karaoke nights "staff meetings" so that all her employees would attend. Without realizing it, Anna was following Tibetan Buddhist Pema Chodron's recommendation to "liberate [yourself] from confusion" by doing "non-habitual" things like singing or dancing.

The truth is many addicts and alcoholics have a tendency to isolate when they're depressed or triggered or tired. While recharging by spending time alone is crucial, there's a fine line between replenishing energy reserves and having an exclusive and seemingly satisfying relationship with Netflix. It's therefore important to prioritize being around other people—whether that means joining a hiking club, soccer league, community theater or church choir. It's even better if you can do it with other people who are in recovery or focused on creating better lives for themselves. This doesn't mean you need to surround yourself with an army of sober people because otherwise you're destined to go off the rails, just that since addicts can get in their heads, it's best not to spend too much time alone.

Here's a tip we've figured out over the years: if you're wondering if you're isolating, you probably are. Think about Rat Park and find your own version of wood chips, platforms, running wheels, tin cans—and, of course, people.

SECTION 3:
Communities for People in Recovery:
The Options Are Endless

There are many avenues to recovery, and while we don't have the space to explore all of them in depth here, we want to provide the basics about some of the more commonly explored avenues.

Twelve-Step Programs

Twelve-step programs are based around people giving up a specific behavior by practicing twelve steps. While there are numerous 12-step programs (see a partial list below), the best known—and one most attended by addicts and alcoholics—is Alcoholics Anonymous (AA). For the uninitiated, AA is a self-supporting organization meant to help problem drinkers find a relationship with a Higher Power of their own understanding. The concept is that this will allow them to find a spiritual way of living that helps them clean up their past, clear their resentments and, in turn, remove the desire to drink and do drugs.

Created in 1935 after a stockbroker named Bill Wilson helped an acquaintance, Dr. Bob, find recovery from chronic alcoholism, AA now has millions of members around the world. While every AA meeting is independently operated by volunteers and all are run with differing formats agreed upon by the group, there are central offices all over the world and a General Service Office in New York that make program decisions based on input from those within AA. Most meetings are based on the book *Alcoholics Anonymous* (commonly referred to as the Big Book), which is currently in its fourth edition.

Some Popular 12-Step Programs Besides AA:

- ACA – Adult Children of Alcoholics
- Alanon – For families and friend of alcoholics
- CA – Cocaine Anonymous
- CMA – Crystal Meth Anonymous
- DA – Debtors Anonymous
- FAA – Food Addicts Anonymous
- GA – Gamblers Anonymous
- HA – Heroin Anonymous
- MA – Marijuana Anonymous
- NA – Narcotics Anonymous
- NicA – Nicotine Anonymous
- OA – Overeaters Anonymous
- SAA – Sex Addicts Anonymous
- SLAA – Sex and Love Addicts Anonymous

12-Step Programs You Had No Idea Existed

- Cleptomaniacs and Shoplifters Anonymous
- Clutterers Anonymous
- Computer Gaming Addicts Anonymous

- Emotions Anonymous
- Liars Anonymous
- Rageaholics Anonymous
- Self-Mutilators Anonymous
- Social Anxiety Anonymous

Non-12-Step Programs For Recovery:

Just because 12-step is the best-known program for recovery, that doesn't make it the only way that addicts and alcoholics can connect with others. Because of various issues people have increasingly had with 12-step over the past few years, these alternative programs have had a surge in popularity. Below, we'll detail some of the other options out there.

Celebrate Recovery

It's safe to say that anyone avoiding 12-step programs because of the concept of a Higher Power won't be the right fit for Celebrate Recovery, a Christ-centered program based around Biblical truth that was launched by Saddleback Church over two decades ago. While Celebrate Recovery also offers twelve steps (with accompanying Scriptures), the program additionally includes eight principles based on the Beatitudes. The goal is to give addicts a "clear path of salvation and discipleship; bringing hope, freedom, sobriety, healing, and the opportunity to give back one day at a time through our one and only true Higher Power, Jesus Christ." At this point, Celebrate Recovery can be found in over 29,000 churches across the world.

L.I.F.E. Recovery

L.I.F.E. Recovery, a support group ministry with a mission to help people live "in integrity," is also Christ-centered. It offers workbook resources, educational multimedia presentations, and support group structure to the Christian community.

SMART Recovery

On the opposite end of the option scale is SMART Recovery (Self-Management and Recovery Training), which is built around four points: Building and Maintaining Motivation; Coping with Urges; Managing Thoughts, Feelings and Behaviors; and Living a Balanced Life. While there are in-person meetings around the world, there are also special events, webinars and regular SMART meetings online.

SOS

Secular Organizations for Sobriety (SOS) is a network of local groups that help people get and stay sober from alcohol, drugs, food and more. Founded in the '80s and based in Hollywood, California, SOS is a non-profit organization with meetings all over the world.

Matrix

The Matrix Model, also launched in the '80s, is a four-month intensive outpatient program for people who want treatment but don't want to check in anywhere. It's supported by the National Institute on Drug Abuse (NIDA), and patients can stay in it for up to a year.

LifeRing

A network meant to help people remain abstinent from alcohol and other non-medically indicated drugs, LifeRing support, much like in 12-step, is peer-to-peer and emphasizes growth and personal empowerment. LifeRing holds face-to-face meetings all over the U.S. and Canada, as well as in several other countries, and also offers meetings online.

Recovery 2.0

Recovery 2.0 is a community that was launched in 2013 by our friend Tommy Rosen, a yoga teacher, spiritual leader, author and person in long-term recovery. It includes online global conferences, coaching programs and retreats, and takes a holistic approach to recovery from addiction of all kinds (drugs, alcohol, sex, food—you name it). While Recovery 2.0 welcomes people who have recovered in whatever way and through whatever program they've found, it places a great deal of emphasis on health and wellness—especially yoga, meditation and nutrition.

Online Meetings

Online meetings have taken off in the past few years. Although a variety of sites provide online meetings, the Mack Daddy is InTheRooms.com, a site where hundreds of thousands of people with a collective million-plus years of sobriety convene. (Sobriety isn't a prerequisite for attendance; there are plenty of people seeking help, as well as family members and friends.) ITR, as it's known, doesn't only offer 12-step meetings but also a variety of other 12-step and non-12-step groups, in addition to daily meditations, afternoon affirmations, apps and more.

SECTION 4:
Contributing and Volunteering

In case volunteering and giving back sounds like a whole bunch of rah-rah, airy-fairy nonsense, know this: there's actual scientific proof that volunteering makes people feel better: a 2017 study of over 2,700 people by United Healthcare and Volunteer Match revealed that 5 percent of U.S. adults feel physically healthier by volunteering. In addition, study participants reported that they felt like they had more control over their health and self-esteem as a result of giving back.

This focus on others can be especially important to those in recovery from addiction since we have often spent years focused solely on ourselves.

How A Trip to an Assisted Living Home Gave Birth to the Uber for Volunteers

When Joe was first putting his life together after recovering from addiction, he got a job selling gym memberships in New Mexico, where he lived with his dad. It was at that gym that he met someone who ran a mental hospital and hired him as a mental health tech. Part of his job involved driving the alcoholics and drug-addicted inpatients to 12-step meetings. He had no idea at the time how much of an impact the principles he was hearing about were having on him, but he did discover how much being of service to other people made him feel better.

It was when he was at an assisted living home for a gratitude dinner for the husband of his dear friend, Dr. Janice Dorn, and saw a lonely man sitting by himself that Joe's whole concept of being of service went to the next level. When he was talking to this man, he realized how many thousands of sad and terminally ill people who had lost all their family members were sitting in nursing homes. He also realized how many people would want to sit and talk with these patients if there was an organized way to find out who needed companionship.

Joe talked about the experience on an episode of the *I Love Marketing* podcast, mentioning that if anyone listening had an idea about how to organize and connect these two groups, they should reach out. Well, someone did. That someone was Chip Frank, a committed listener who then went and launched a company called Joe Volunteer, which he named in honor of Joe. It's essentially an Uber for volunteering, where people are connected with the organizations that need them and so any "average Joe," male or female, can volunteer at assisted living homes, recovery clinics, nursing homes, children's hospitals, animal shelters, burn units, homeless shelters or disaster relief centers. Being helpful to others, Joe knows, provides hope without you having to do anything except be useful.

When in Doubt, Do the Dishes

When Anna was new to sobriety, she struggled when going home to visit her family. There was something about being in the environment where she'd spent her formative years that caused her to emotionally regress and begin behaving the way she'd acted as a teenager. She was irritable and tempestuous—essentially, the same person she'd been when she started drinking and doing drugs. When she complained to a friend about this, the friend told her that the people who install your buttons are the best people at pushing them. She figured that was that and surrendered to the notion of being a door-slamming adolescent during those visits.

Then someone she knew in recovery asked her why she felt she got so rattled when she was around her family. Anna muttered something about how her family didn't treat her the way she felt she deserved to be treated; she listed a litany of examples. That friend pointed out that she was spending a whole lot of time focusing on what she needed and wasn't getting. "Of course," Anna said. "How are you going to get what you need if you don't figure out what it is?"

"But it doesn't seem like thinking about that is making you feel very good," the friend pointed out. "Why don't you try to shift your focus when you're home to what you can give to the situation rather than what you're not getting?"

And so that became Anna's *raison d'être* during every trip home; each time she saw an opportunity to contribute to a situation, she took it—whether that meant filling up her Mom's car with gas or asking her parents about their lives instead of yammering on about her own. Most of the time, it just meant offering to do the dishes. The process made little sense to her—how could soaping up some plates and then putting them in a dishwasher transform the emotional tenor of her entire visit?—but there was no denying the fact that it worked. She realized that it was the constant focus on herself that was keeping her so agitated; magically, as soon as she stopped trying to get what she felt she needed from her family, she found that they were giving her exactly that.

It's Easy: Just Do the Opposite of What You Want To

"Contrary action" is a popular concept in the recovery world. The thinking behind it is that addicts can sometimes, even in recovery, tend toward self-destructiveness. That self-destructiveness may take the form of obsessive cookie eating or *Game of Thrones* marathons (or far more dangerous distractions), but addictive thinking can make people want to wallow in discomfort or misery to the point that we're almost bathing in it.

When we're in that state, all we have to do, they tell us, is the opposite of what we want to. When we think, "Don't pick up the phone when it rings," we need to pick up the phone. When our first thought is, "Skipping the gym yesterday didn't feel terrible; I might as well try skipping it again today," we need to get out the running shoes. Of course, despite the fact that we're given this direction over and over again, some of us can have extremely short memories (it's no wonder that people have said that the "ism" part of the word "alcoholism" stands for Incredibly Short Memory). Luckily, we have sponsors and friends in recovery who are there to remind us to get out of the house when we most feel like shutting ourselves in.

RECOVERY WARRIOR MORNING ROUTINE

LISA SMITH
FACEBOOK.COM/LISASMITH
TWITTER/INSTAGRAM: @GIRLWALKSOUT

Lisa is a writer and lawyer in New York City. She is the author of *Girl Walks Out of a Bar*, her award-winning memoir of high-functioning addiction and recovery in the world of New York City corporate law.

Sober for more than a decade, Lisa is passionate about breaking the stigma of addiction and mental health issues. She is a frequent speaker on the subject, particularly to audiences of lawyers and other professionals. Her writing has been published in *The Washington Post*, *Chicago Tribune*, AfterPartyMagazine.com, and Addiction.com. She has also appeared on *Megyn Kelly TODAY* and *BBC World News* discussing alcoholism.

Prior to beginning her more than fifteen-year legal marketing career, Lisa practiced law in the corporate finance group of a leading international firm. She is a graduate of Northwestern University and Rutgers School of Law, where she served on the editorial board of the *Rutgers Law Review*. Lisa serves on the board of directors of The Writers Room in New York City. She lives in New York City with her husband, Craig.

Lisa's morning routine:

- I'm most productive in the morning, so I get up between 4:30 and 5:30 a.m.

- I love being awake before the sun comes up, and I light a candle near my desk for soft lighting.

- First things first means coffee for me, so I make a hot blended concoction with maca powder, protein and coconut milk. Straight caffeine on an empty stomach doesn't work for me, and this combination goes easy on my stomach. It also kick-starts my brain.

- While the coffee brews, I lie on the floor and do stretches for my back. I have degenerative spinal stenosis, so it's important for me to do a lot of stretching. It's particularly helpful first thing in the morning.

- Over coffee, I skim my emails, social media and favorite news sources to catch up on anything I missed after going to bed early the night before (another regular habit).

- I put on my headphones (New York City is noisy even that early!) and do a twenty-minute guided meditation. I have vivid dreams and often wake up thinking about them, as well as what I need to do that day; meditation stops that thought loop and connects me to the present moment. It clears my head.

- Depending on the day, I'll spend the next hour or two on one of three things: 1) a 12-step meeting near my office; 2) working out, which means thirty minutes of cardio and thirty minutes of strengthening, mostly around my core in order to help my back; or 3) writing, either working on something related to upcoming speaking engagements or a personal essay.

- Whichever of these activities I'm doing, I time it so that I can be at the law firm where I work near Times Square by 8:30. Given how hectic both the job and the area are, I like being there and settled in before everyone else arrives, closer to 9:00 or 9:30. It gives me time to get my head around the day, prepare for meetings and not feel rushed.

- I am a creature of routine, and my morning routine is key to giving me a calm and relaxed mindset that helps me throughout the day. It also feels great to be productive early and take care of important things that keep me sober and healthy. I get into the office feeling like I've already accomplished something, which means less pressure for the rest of the day!

— 8 —

LEVEL 10 RECOVERY SKILL #2:

CLEAN UP YOUR BODY

""They say you are what you eat, so I strive to be healthy
My goal in life is not to be rich or wealthy
'Cause true wealth comes from good health and wise ways
We got to start taking better care of ourselves."

—DEAD PREZ

If you're coming from a life of active addiction and have finally given up repeatedly doing something that was killing you, cleaning up your diet may be the last thing you want to do. You may feel like you're depriving yourself of plenty already. But if you can start to look at healthy living and a clean diet as a gift and not a sacrifice, you may be surprised how much better you can feel.

As the saying goes, why would you switch seats on the Titanic? In other words, why break one bad habit that was killing you only to risk letting another?

SECTION 1: Diet and Exercise

If Addicts Don't Fix the Gut, They Can Stay Stuck

Joe takes clean eating to impressive heights, having given up caffeine and cane sugar starting in 2016. But his belief in the importance of healthy eating in order to fix the gut, particularly for those in recovery, goes far beyond his own experience.

He first became enlightened about the importance of healthy eating for addicts when he met a doctor named David Arneson in the fall of 2016. Arneson, who has treated over 20,000 addicts over nearly two decades with IV treatments, explained to Joe that many homeless addicts are living with modern-day scurvy because of their poor diet. As a result, their bodies are not producing enough serotonin, which means that they stay in a constant craving state.

Because of that, Arneson started administering IV treatments of amino acids, vitamin C and B vitamins to help addicts in that situation rebuild their microbiome (the ecosystem of bacteria in our body, the majority of which are in our digestive system). After up to twelve weeks of treatments, he discovered, they were able to produce serotonin again and their hormones were regulated, which in turn made them much more likely to start attending recovery meetings, seeing therapists and working on their trauma. As Arneson explained to Joe, the gut is the "second brain" since 70 percent of serotonin is produced there.

This doesn't mean, of course, that every addict needs to get injected with IVs or eliminate sugar. But if you've gotten to the point where you need hospitalization or medical care for addiction, treating your gut will have a massive impact on the effectiveness of treating your mind.

The Burpee Habit

Fitness is a major part of life for both of us. While we've each exercised regularly since getting into recovery, Joe's exercise regime went through a major shift the day he met Joe De Sena, the creator of Spartan Races, in early 2017.

Spartan, for the uninitiated, is a series of obstacle races where people climb walls, throw spears and do other impossible-sounding things for up to marathon distances. The races have become nothing short of a sensation, airing on television networks all over the world.

De Sena and Joe decided to interview each other for their respective podcasts, which just happened to be during a time when Joe had a sinus staph infection. In between the two interviews, De Sena announced that the two of them should do burpees (for those who don't know, burpees, sometimes called squat thrusts, start with the person in a standing position, then move to squats, then a plank, then back to a squat and then back to standing). Joe explained that he had a cold, to which De Sena replied that if any of the Spartan Race participants don't complete any of the obstacles, they're required to do thirty burpees before continuing the race.

This was enough to motivate Joe, who, despite his cold, ended up doing sixty burpees in a row with De Sena. Although he felt like dying at certain points throughout the process, he also became committed. If race participants could do thirty burpees while also enduring some of the most grueling exercise imaginable, Joe reasoned he could do at least that many every morning. (As of this writing, he was doing between 30 and 120 every day, oftentimes between sets of weight lifting—a commitment Anna can vouch for since he makes her do them with him when she visits him.)

What, exactly, makes Joe so passionate about burpees? As far as he sees it, a burpee is an ideal form of exercise because it doesn't require any equipment, adds to the intensity of whatever workout you're already doing and, much like drug addiction, gets less intense over time as you build up a tolerance. In this case, though, that's a positive thing.

They're also, Joe says, an ideal way to quickly give yourself a natural high.

What a Long, Strange Workout It's Been

For as long as she can remember, Anna has been workout-obsessed. She was put in ballet when she was five years old and, by the time she was in high school, was taking pointe classes five times a week and performing in *The Nutcracker*. Her exercise habits continued outside of the ballet studio, as she regularly hit the local aerobics studio (it was the '80s, people) and began choreographing and performing in her high school dance shows and musicals.

Every fitness trend that came along, she embraced—including step, slide (anyone else remember that one?) and spinning. She was the one working out to Jane Fonda's VHS tape in her college dorm.

Even when addiction had her staying up for days at a time, doing cocaine, chugging vodka and chain-smoking, she kept up her exercise habit. Her rule for balancing chain-smoking with workout fanaticism was that she couldn't smoke once she put on her workout clothes, thinking it would make her smoke less. (In case you're wondering, it didn't work; she'd just change clothes.)

After thirteen years of smoking, Anna finally quit in July of 2001, and that's when her devotion to fitness hit full force. A self-proclaimed "ADD exerciser," Anna tends to get terribly excited about a certain form of exercise, do it passionately for anywhere between a few months to a few years, and then move on (thank God she's living in the ClassPass era). She can describe in detail the various forms of barre classes and passionately debate whether "old school" spinning is better than the SoulCycle version. Unfortunately for her wallet, the only type of exercise that Anna seems not to like is the kind that's free—say, running.

Among the wackier workouts she's tried over the years are GST (which stands for Grace Somatomorphic Technique, a "fascia body conditioning system" that is taught at an LA studio and is sort of like Pilates, sort of like yoga and sort of like a stretching class but really not like any other exercise Anna has ever tried before), Rise Nation (which incorporates elements of spinning, wall climbing and a step machine) and Power Plate (where you stand on a vibrating platform—yes, really— while doing exercises for greater impact). Anna also loves her dance classes and some comparatively normal workouts like hot yoga and Pilates.

Because Anna's a class devotee, she can't always control when in the day she exercises. And so, on the days when she doesn't go to a class in the morning, she incorporates a bit of exercise into her Miracle Morning: after walking around the block, she comes back inside and does fifty quick jumping jacks while looking at one of her two vision boards. By feeling the blood rushing through her veins, she then feels like she's truly earned that first cup of coffee.

SECTION 2: Alternative Medicine

Every Treatment Method You Can Think of—And Then Some More

Truth talk: there's almost nothing we haven't experimented with when it comes to healing and treating the body. We both regularly have massages and acupuncture and have also both tried EMDR, EFT (tapping), Transcendental Meditation, biofeedback, cryotherapy, floating and several other techniques. And Joe may be the only person alive who's had his brain scanned six times by world-renowned brain disorder specialist Dr. Daniel Amen, simply to explore what's going on in his brain.

So, what are some of these treatments?

EMDR stands for Eye Movement Desensitization and Reprocessing and is a psychotherapy treatment designed to diminish stress associated with trauma. It involves thinking about traumatic memories while also focusing on external stimuli (usually hand tapping or audio stimulation). The idea is that new associations are made between the trauma so that it stops having a debilitating impact on the client.

Biofeedback involves electrodes that are strapped to your skin and send signals to a monitor, which tracks heart rate, blood pressure and more. Because you can get real-time analysis of stress levels, you're able to practice relaxation techniques in the moment and see on the monitor how effective they are.

Cryotherapy is where you expose yourself to temperatures below minus 100 degrees. For whole body cryotherapy, you step into cryotherapy chambers for between two and four minutes (while wearing very little—usually nothing but socks, underwear, mittens, ear muffs, a hat and a face mask). It's used not only to treat swollen muscles but also for mood. Anna was first introduced to cryotherapy when *Vice* magazine assigned her a story on it. Attracted to anything that claimed to burn thousands of calories in just a few minutes, she embraced the assignment and went charging into a booth that was

200 degrees below 0 at a local cryotherapy place. While she can't say that she noticed those calories disappearing, she did end up leaning on cryotherapy during the month after her cat died and a romantic relationship broke up. And she found that freezing her body for a little over two minutes had an undeniable impact on her mood. Science backs up her experience: a 2008 study followed a group of eighteen- to sixty-five-year-olds suffering from depression and anxiety who showed more improvement after three weeks of daily, two- to three-minute cryogenic treatments than a control group.

Floating involves going into a floatation tank filled with water and enough Epsom salts to make you, well, float. Floatation tanks, which are usually light- and sound-proof, have recently (like cryotherapy) become all the rage in terms of helping people de-stress, sleep better and diminish pain—which means that of course both Anna and Joe have tried them. After putting in ear plugs, clients lie in tanks for up to ninety minutes, the last twenty of which ideally involves being in the state that tends to occur just before sleep and when waking, but without the person losing consciousness. Lest you question Joe's dedication to floating, know this: he keeps a floatation tank manufactured by Nick Janicki, the world's leading float pod expert, in his office and is currently working with Janicki on building recovery-related audio books into float pods. Joe tries to float once a week because it adds a level of peace and serenity that he doesn't seem to otherwise get. As he says, if you don't manage modern life, it will manage you, and one of the best things we can do is build in ways to be able to just be by ourselves without any sort of stimulation.

Joe has also done thirty-five sessions of hyperbaric oxygen therapy (HBOT), which involves wearing an oxygen bubble on your head so your body is forced to get oxygenated in order to promote healing. He did it at the recommendation of Dr. Daniel Amen, ten-time *New York Times* bestselling author and the world's leading brain expert, who scanned his brain and determined that he had frontal lobe damage. The reason this is relevant for addicts is that the brains of addicts show up differently under scans than those of non-addicts. Of course, there are many factors that could cause an unhealthy brain—including trauma, injuries and environmental poisoning—but addiction is among them. Luckily, good nutrition, exercise, sleep and clean living can change that.

Meditation: The Game-Changer of All Game-Changers

Without a doubt, the most significant "alternative therapy" that we've both embraced is meditation.

Anna went to a Vedic Meditation lecture in the early 2000s only because she was supposed to have dinner with a friend who changed the plan at the last minute and invited her along to the talk. (As discussed earlier, Vedic Meditation is a mantra-based offshoot of Transcendental Meditation, or TM.) Then she heard the teacher, Thom Knoles, address all the things that a regular meditation practice could do; he talked about how humans are wired to be flooded with enough adrenaline to fight off wild boars and, since we don't need that sort of adrenaline in modern life, our bodies have accumulated volumes of excess stress. Think about when you're driving, he said, and the driver in front of you slams on the brakes, causing you to think for a split second that you're about to crash. Your system is flooded with "wild boar fighting" adrenaline, and all that stress just stays there—until you learn to do things like meditate. He said that since meditation is 10 times more restful than sleep, meditators can get up earlier and accomplish more. But he really got her attention when he said that meditation can help slow down the aging process. By the end of the lecture, Anna had committed to receiving her mantra from him the next day.

Still, she surprised herself with how much she took to the practice, immediately implementing it into her daily routine for twenty minutes every morning and another twenty in the afternoon. It turned out that the mantra Knoles had given her calmed her previously restless mind, and his method—which emphasizes accepting when your mind wanders rather than shaming yourself for it—worked for her. She's been doing it ever since, and though she admits that she has definitely missed her second practice of the day, she rarely has a fully meditation-free day. A few years after receiving her mantra from Knoles, she went back and received an "advanced one"—which is five syllables instead of three—and has practiced with that one since.

While Vedic Meditation is her focus, Anna has also tried various other forms of meditation over the years—including Buddhist—and been on meditation retreats at Esalen Institute and Spirit Rock Meditation Center in California.

Joe learned Transcendental Meditation when he went to Fairfield, Iowa, in 2013 with Brendon Burchard to receive an award from Maharishi University for his contributions in entrepreneurship. They both underwent a four-day training where they were given individual mantras, and while Joe admits to "falling off the wagon" at times, on good meditation days, he'll meditate for twenty minutes every morning and twenty minutes every afternoon.

And Then There's Just Breathing

Some people believe that recovery from addiction happens in the foot-long area between your mouth and stomach. And it doesn't take a doctor to know that the most anxious people have shallow breathing. Joe, who has done Kundalini yoga with Tommy Rosen, starts the day with a breathing practice and then periodically reminds himself to take five deep breaths whenever it occurs to him throughout the day. He also uses various breathing apps like Spire and HeartMath, an app and sensor device, and has occasionally practiced Wim Hof breathing techniques (which is similar to inner heat and yogic breathing and has been likened to controlled hyperventilating).

The Controversy Around Spirituality

Spirituality—and most especially religion—is a highly-debated topic within the recovery community. Plenty of struggling addicts stay away from 12-step programs out of the belief that this will mean having to get really into the "God thing." While Joe and Anna both know plenty of atheists within the 12-step community, embracing spiritual principles changed the game for Anna when it came to finding recovery—and serenity.

While she'd never had a problem believing in the notion of God before she went to rehab, it wasn't a concept she thought about much.

Then she was introduced to the idea that a Higher Power could help relieve her of her obsession to do cocaine and drink. She was desperate, so she was willing to try this ridiculous-sounding concept. She followed other people's directions to write out her ideas of what this Higher Power could be and became willing to do things she never had been willing to do before—such as pray to that Higher Power on her knees. Slowly, through this practice—and through regularly thinking about the idea that there was a benign something out there that only wanted what was best for her—she could take the pressure off her own obsession with controlling everything. Her life started to improve. Quickly, she noticed something shocking: she had no desire to drink or do drugs. She felt like she'd experienced something similar before when, at the age of 19, she'd had her tonsils—a part of her that didn't work—removed; in this case, her obsession with doing drugs and drinking had been extracted. Except there had been no operation. Since that didn't make logical sense—she'd tried to quit many, many times and nothing had worked—she had to assume the solution had been spiritual.

She doesn't claim to understand anything beyond that, but she knows that when she remembers there's something larger than her out there and that this whatever-it-is has a better idea of what's good for her than she often does for herself, she feels better. (It's easier said than done, and plenty of times she finds herself off the spiritual beam but, with few exceptions, her desire to do drugs and drink has been gone since the fall of 2000.)

Joe's spiritual beliefs are very tied into connecting with other people. His whole life, he often says, is about trying to deepen his connection with himself, which in turn helps him deepen his connection with other people. His desire for connection may come from a dark place—from feeling profoundly disconnected as a child and then later as a drug addict—but he's been able to turn that deficit into his greatest strength.

It's no wonder he's often called the world's best connector; connection is literally what helps keep Joe alive. And, we both believe, it's more important for people in recovery than for any other group of people in the world.

RECOVERY WARRIOR MORNING ROUTINE

STEPHEN DANSIGER

FACEBOOK.COM/DRSTEPHENDANSIGER

INSTAGRAM/TWITTER: @DRDANSIGER

Stephen Dansiger, PsyD, MFT, played CBGB and Max's Kansas City in the late '70s; drank and played drums in a toy rock band; got sober in the late '80s; and became an international educator and rocker again in the '90s, followed by a sought-after clinician, writer and meditation teacher in the 2000s. On top of attempting to cure Marc Maron on *WTF*, Dr. Steve has also become a master EMDR therapist and provider of EMDR Basic Training and Advanced Topics courses with the Institute for Creative Mindfulness, and helped set up the premiere Buddhist informed addiction rehab center, Refuge Recovery Center. He has been practicing Buddhist mindfulness for almost thirty years (including a one-year residency at a Zen monastery) and teaches dharma classes regularly at Against the Stream Buddhist Meditation Society in Los Angeles and other centers nationally and internationally. His second book (co-authored with Dr. Jamie Marich), *EMDR Therapy and Mindfulness for Trauma-Focused Car*e, is available now from Springer Publishing Company.

Stephen's morning routine:

- The morning has been my favorite part of the day ever since I got sober (well, okay, maybe it took me a few weeks to get there, but ever since after those first few cloudy weeks). My morning routine has changed over the last almost thirty years of recovery, but one element has remained the same: I start early.

- I am up between 4:30 a.m. and 5 a.m. That started even before I lived at a Zen monastery, where the wake-up call is earlier. I have found that I am at my best at this time of day, so I want to use as many of these hours as possible. It starts with me rolling out of bed and on to the meditation cushion, with the goal of meditating for at least half an hour. If that isn't possible because of the day's schedule, I just reduce the time based on what I can do, which helps make the cushion time itself non-negotiable. Next, I put on the coffee and sit down to three pages of free writing in the fashion of Julia Cameron's *The Artist's Way*, a book I first worked with in early recovery. I have been doing these morning pages now for most of the last twenty-five years or so. Julia recommends they be done before anything else, but I have found at this point it works better for me when they follow my mindfulness practice. Then, if I am currently working on a writing project, I will give myself a word count and dedicate some of this time to writing.

- Next, I sit with my daily planner, one of the many new ones on the market, which helps organize my thinking for the day from this more relaxed and spiritual perspective. I check in with gratitude, enjoy what is exciting up ahead, lean into my positive self-talk for the week, set priorities, and update my schedule. Then, regardless of any other physical exercise that I am able to fit in during the morning or later in the day, I do some light yoga, along with sit-ups and push-ups, making sure that moving my body is part of every day.

- Then comes my favorite part of the morning routine that is the result of the changes in my life in sobriety. It's time to wake up my (now) 8-year-old daughter and get her ready for school. I am her morning drop-off person. Instead of believing it be a hassle, the rest of my morning routine and other spiritual practice have taught me these are some of my most precious minutes with her. After she is fed and dressed, we usually play together a bit and then talk in the car unless she wants to be contemplative. The parent community is strong at her school, so I make a point to see some of my parent friends before I head back to my car. This is absolutely part of my morning routine. My first relational moments are family- and community-oriented.

- As a result of my early wake-up, it is now only 8:15 a.m., and I am generally feeling spiritually fit for the day. I have arranged my work schedule so that often I have some more time available to work on a writing project, see a friend for coffee, or any number of possibilities. Either way, without my morning routine, I don't know how I would do anything that follows in the day. It doesn't always roll out perfectly, but if I am vigilant about not getting pulled away by the phone or social media, I can feed myself in this way most every day.

— 9 —

Level 10 Recovery Skill #3:

CLEAR YOUR MIND

"Free your mind
And the rest will follow."
—EN VOGUE

Once we get drugs, alcohol and addictive thinking out of our bodies and minds, we still often have work to do—namely, working with a mind that drove us to do these things to excess in the first place.

While opinions vary on the matter, plenty of people believe that addicts are more sensitive than non-addicts. Whether we're born that way, become that way as a result of our life circumstances or some combination of those two things, the thinking is that the realities of life feel a bit too harsh for us. What can hurt our feelings or bother us may not impact non-addicts at all. As a result, we use drugs, alcohol, sex, drugs, food, gambling or any other addictive behavior as an escape.

And just because we get into recovery doesn't mean we are given new brains. Our brains are just cleared of toxic chemicals, in the case of alcohol and drug addiction.

The rest of the brain-clearing is up to us.

SECTION 1:
The Tendency to Overreact

Addicts, even those in recovery, have been described as people with their fists metaphorically braced for battle. We can have a "get them before they get me" attitude, subconsciously believing that the world is stacked against us and taking anything—from the way the barista looks at us to our co-worker's mood one afternoon—personally.

In short, we can get "in our heads" and then overreact to situations in ways that we later regret.

How to Practice Non-Reaction

There's a popular expression in recovery circles: "Pause when agitated."

In our experience, there may be no more important three-word combination. Anna, in particular, has been well-served by this aphorism. As she sees it, she's always been an incredibly reactive person, unable to not respond if she feels triggered. But she noticed something once she got into recovery: she couldn't always trust her mind. She discovered that there was a reason she turned to drugs and alcohol at such a young age: her brain is naturally awash with extreme thoughts. Things and people are the "best" or the "worst." And if someone does something she finds upsetting, her brain often tells her she has to deal with it right then.

The problem is, oftentimes there's nothing to deal with. Oftentimes, her reaction is actually an overreaction. Another popular recovery expression is: "When it's hysterical, it's historical"—which is to say that when we have an extreme reaction to something relatively minor, it's probably because this small thing is reminding us, internally, of a previously experienced "big thing."

We've heard people say that the amount of time addicts in recovery are able to pause is directly proportional to their years in recovery—after a year, they can pause for a second, after two years, two seconds, and so on. The important thing is to be able to feel triggered, acknowledge that you're having a reaction, and then take a break to ask yourself four very important words: "How important is it?" There are some great follow-ups to that question, such as: "Is it worth getting more upset?" and "Is my reaction going to make the situation better?" Usually, the answers are "no" and "no."

Another popular recovery expression is that we should practice "restraint of pen and tongue." (Or, in modern parlance, "restraint of pen, tongue, keyboard, and Siri.") This means that when Anna gets the enraging email that she feels like she has to respond to right then, the last thing she actually needs to do is respond to that email. There's a specific equation to follow: the more she feels she has to respond right then, the more important it is for her *not* to respond right then. If she literally cannot stop herself from responding, she writes the email and attempts to not send it until she's slept on it (even better if she can send it to someone who's not involved in the situation to get feedback; inevitably, that person will suggest that rather than revising it, she just delete it. For the record, Anna is probably successful in this only 64 percent of the time).

Would You Talk to a Child the Way You Talk to Yourself?

A few years into recovery, Anna noticed something: she told herself some pretty nasty things. If she screwed something up, she might call herself an idiot. If she felt bad, she'd sometimes tell herself that she *always* felt bad (despite tangible evidence to the contrary). If someone didn't smile back at her when she showed them her pearly whites, she'd immediately assume that person disliked her.

One day, she asked herself: if I was taking care of a small child and she made a mistake or felt bad or didn't get a smile back, would I tell her that she was an idiot, always felt bad or was probably disliked? The answer, of course, was no. Then she had to ask herself an even tougher question: if she wouldn't talk to someone who didn't actually exist in such a cruel way, why was she doing it to the person she spent the most of her time with and whom she most needed to love?

The problem was that her regular thoughts had become so entangled with those self-critical ones that she had trouble even recognizing when the cruel ones were coming through. The ultimate solution she found was to notice when she was feeling bad and then take out a notebook and jot down whatever she was thinking at that moment. Eventually, she had a list that she called Mean Things I Say to Myself. Having it in black and white on a page didn't immediately stop her from the nasty habit, but it made her aware. It was years later that she realized her thoughts about herself had become quite loving. She's not sure where those cruel thoughts went. They might just be living in that notebook.

SECTION 2: Anger and Depression

Having a Resentment Is Like Drinking Poison and Expecting the Other Person to Die

As some people know, one of the twelve steps involves making a list of the people at whom you're angry. Anna was thrilled when she got to this step; she'd been waiting her whole life for someone to listen to the entire list of people who had wronged her. And now, because of the program, she'd found she could get someone to do this—and for free! She eagerly sat down to write out her list, starting with her first resentment (age four, when she got her friend Shawna a Christmas present, but Shawna didn't get her one) and ending with a resentment she'd copped probably the day she made the list. In the end, her notebook contained hundreds of names and misdeeds, and she felt extremely convinced of the fact that they had all wronged her.

But when she shared this list with her sponsor, the sponsor pointed out something gleaned from 12-step literature: in nearly every one of her resentments, Anna played a part. In some cases, she'd actually done something to produce the result she resented (say, yelling at her boss before getting fired and then resenting him for having fired her). In other situations, she merely resented someone for behaving in a way she didn't like—for saying no to her when she thought they should say yes. Rather than accepting what had happened as for the best or just how things were, her ego helped her come up with stories that proved how wrong the person who'd committed the act in question was.

For years, she believed that her self-righteous anger at all those people made her feel much better. She had been right, after all, and the other person had been wrong. But once all those resentments were on the page and she was talking about them, she realized that hating those people was only making her feel worse.

She was the one who was uncomfortable if she ever saw or thought about the person.

She was the one wasting mental space on something that had happened minutes or hours or months or years or decades before.

And, in doing that, she was keeping herself a victim. She was thinking of herself as someone bad things happened to. In owning her part in those resentments, she was able to step out of victimhood and realize that, sure, people had done bad things to her in some cases but she'd also done bad things to other people. It was part of being human and learning lessons. She saw that the sooner it was possible to let go of resentments (sometimes quickly, sometimes slowly), the sooner she could feel better. And something interesting happened the more she practiced letting go: she had fewer resentments.

The So-Called Luxury of Anger

Despite how much Anna was able to quell her resentments, she wasn't able to rid herself of anger. Let's just say that Anna has always been, well, quite in touch with the angry side of her personality. Then she heard people in recovery meetings talk about anger as a luxury— as something they could use so long as they could handle it.

Just hearing about this concept motivated Anna to examine her relationship with anger. She knew people who could lose it and then seemingly revert back to whatever emotion they were experiencing before. Anna couldn't. When she got angry, she stayed angry. To her, it was like cocaine—once she started, it was really hard to stop. So she made a decision: if she ever found herself in a situation where she could decide whether or not to get angry (or angrier), she would pick not to. It's a drug, she's realized, that she can't use in moderation.

And then there's narcissism. While Anna clearly isn't the only person in the world who's struggled with this issue, she always excelled at thinking somewhat obsessively about herself—and often about the ways she felt she'd been wronged. It was a great epiphany when she entered recovery and realized that one of the reasons she was so unhappy was because she thought of herself so much of the time. "I'm not much, but I'm all I think about" is an expression she heard at one of her first recovery meetings, and she clung to it.

The concept that self-obsession makes us unhappy isn't terribly complicated. Neither of us are mathematicians, but we both agree on the fact that the more you think about your life, the more unhappy you're going to be. As they say in 12-step rooms, "figure it out" isn't one of the twelve steps. In other words, the solution to a so-called problem may be to stop thinking about it.

SECTION 3:
Fear, Self-Obsession and the Desire to Control

Addicts don't own the patent on character defects. We do, however, often have a great many issues to work through—issues that have manifested themselves in qualities that make us unhappy. Some people say that our defects are what helped us survive addiction and recovering involves finding new tools.

We have discovered a myriad of new tools over the years, but it involved first facing what was causing us pain.

Fear—Otherwise Known as False Evidence Appearing Real

Early on in recovery, Anna heard people talking about how alcoholics and addicts live with "100 forms of fear." She metaphorically checked "N/A" on that concept, telling herself that she wasn't scared of anything. After all, she reasoned, she went on live TV without her pulse racing, and she'd gone skydiving and rappelled down a building.

But fear, she learned over time, was craftier than she was. She realized that it didn't always come up as the thought, "I'm scared." Her psyche had somehow internalized that she wasn't allowed to feel fear; that fear was for weak people. And in not allowing herself to feel it, fear had festered, to the point that it only made itself known in disguise: as the feeling that she was sad or sick or indifferent.

Today, she acknowledges that in many ways, she's actually addicted to fear. Her brain manufactures fearful thoughts, and it's her job to remind herself that one acronym for fear is "False Evidence Appearing Real" and another is "F Everything and Run." But there's another one people on fear-combating missions also like: "Face Everything and Recover."

Remembering that fear has many faces can be particularly important to recall first thing in the morning. That's why Anna reads something spiritual before she even starts meditating. The practice reminds her that filling her mind with something positive will set her off on a far better foot than allowing her day to start with whatever detritus her subconscious mind has kicked up. Yet just in case her head is still filled with fear, she has the Rumi quote, "Live life like it's rigged in your favor," written on a chalkboard in her kitchen.

Combating a fear-filled mind isn't always easy, particularly when that fear is wearing a highly deceptive mask. And addicts do seem to be more prone to fear than non-addicts. Fighting fear can be a full-time job for a little while but after your brain gets used to pausing and then re-assessing the so-called scary situation from a calmer perspective, that false evidence stops appearing so real.

How to Get Out of Self-Obsession

Not to state the obvious, but drowning yourself in chemicals means neglecting a great deal of your life, including the other people in it. In other words, addicts certainly aren't the only self-obsessed people in the world, but many of them do relate to feeling like "the piece of crap in the center of the universe"—fueled by a steady combination of self-obsession and self-hatred.

It can, therefore, be something of a process to get into the habit of thinking about other people. But we've both learned repeatedly that whenever we can help other people, it makes us feel better. Joe, especially, notices the impact that volunteering has on his mood. Whenever he's feeling depressed or anxious, he tries to be of service to someone else. In the end, service work can actually be a selfish act: it makes the person doing it feel infinitely better.

The Illusion of Control

Many people in recovery talk about how they're control freaks. Drug addicts, in particular, discuss how they did drugs out of a desire to control how they felt at all times.

In recovery, we can still often have the desire to make our experiences unfold exactly as we'd like. As *Alcoholics Anonymous*, the book used as the basic literature for AA, states:

Each person is like an actor who wants to run the whole show; is forever trying to arrange the lights, the ballet, the scenery and the rest of the players in his own way. If his arrangements would only stay put, if only people would do as he wished, the show would be great. Everybody, including himself, would be pleased. Life would be wonderful. In trying to make these arrangements our actor may sometimes be quite virtuous. He may be kind, considerate, patient, generous; even modest and self-sacrificing. On the other hand, he may be mean, egotistical, selfish and dishonest. But, as with most humans, he is more likely to have varied traits.

What usually happens? The show doesn't come off very well. He begins to think life doesn't treat him right. He decides to exert himself more. He becomes, on the next occasion, still more demanding or gracious, as the case may be. Still the play does not suit him. Admitting he may be somewhat at fault, he is sure that other people are more to blame. He becomes angry, indignant, self-pitying.

While the book isn't speaking only of alcoholics and addicts, it emphasizes the fact that learning to become a "worker among workers" is crucial for people like us. Eventually, we all have to accept the fact that life isn't going to play out exactly as we've scripted it. Because addicts can tend to obsessively focus on the negative, it's even more important for us.

It's no accident that many meetings end with the Serenity Prayer: "God, grant me the serenity to accept the things I can't change, the courage to change the things I can and the wisdom to know the difference."

Here's another quote that works when it comes to surrendering what we want without leaving claw marks on it—this one from the late psychiatrist and spiritual leader David Hawkins: "We get what we want when we stop insisting on it."

RECOVERY WARRIOR MORNING ROUTINE

TARYN STRONG
FACEBOOK.COM/SHERECOVERS
INSTAGRAM: @TARYNSTRONG

Taryn Strong is grateful to be in recovery from drug addiction, self-harm, trauma, disordered eating and codependency. She is the co-creator (with her mom) of the popular online and in-person recovery community She Recovers. Founded in 2011, She Recovers is now the largest female cyber-recovery community in North America. A yoga teacher since 2007, Taryn developed a unique "Yoga for Recovery" program, which integrates yoga and meditation with spirituality and recovery principles from a wide variety of recovery pathways (including but not limited to the 12-step pathway). In addition to teaching yoga classes across Victoria and leading the Yoga for Recovery program for She Recovers retreats, Taryn is currently completing training to become a professional recovery coach.

Taryn's morning routine:

- Before I even open my eyes, I start with gratitude. I fill my entire body with the feeling of gratitude as I think about the wonderful things and people I am grateful for. Next, I meditate. My morning meditation is a mindfulness meditation—I practice staying as present as possible for ten to thirty minutes. This is super important for me because when I wake up, my mind tries to tell me to go straight to my phone to check my emails, social media, plan my day, etc.

- The next part of my morning routine is spent at my altar. My altar is my favorite place in my home. All sorts of wonderful things live on it, including my crystals, tarot cards, and an essential oil diffuser. I pick which oils I want to diffuse that day and put them in my diffuser. I select the oils based on what I need that day—say, either grounding oils, relaxing oils or energizing oils. Then, I pull some oracle/tarot cards, which provide affirmations, clarity and focus for my day.

- Next, I head to the kitchen, crank some tunes and usually have a little solo dance party while I get the kettle ready for my morning hot water and lemon. After that, it's COFFEE time. I sip my coffee while I check my emails and start planning the day.

- (A lot of people are surprised to hear that yoga is not a part of my daily morning routine! Yoga is one of my non-negotiable daily self-care activities, but I love going to the afternoon or evening classes when I practice!)

— 10 —

Level 10 Recovery Skill #4:

BLOW UP YOUR CAREER

"Every day women and men become legends."
—COMMON

SECTION 1:
What Recovery Can Do for a Career

It would be an understatement to say that we weren't successful before recovery. Joe was smoking pot daily by the time he was in high school and smoking coke by the time he was eighteen. He worked throughout his childhood—painting curbs, cleaning out aquariums, delivering papers and pizzas, and eventually dealing drugs. Anna, meanwhile, was fired from most of her early jobs—including her first one, at a yogurt shop where, her boss informed her, she didn't know how to swirl the yogurt correctly. In short, until they got into recovery, neither of them could get anywhere career-wise.

The Problem Wasn't Joe's Industry—It Was Him

Once Joe cleaned up and was selling gym memberships and then working at a mental hospital, a friend of his from high school talked him into starting a carpet cleaning business. Joe knew nothing about cleaning carpets and, as it turned out, even less about what it would be like to be in business with someone who was drinking and using drugs. Soon, Joe let go of the business partner and eventually accumulated $30,000 in debt, trying to run a business that wasn't working.

One day, a different friend from high school invited him on a jet skiing trip. Just like anyone who's $30,000 in debt would feel, Joe hesitated because he didn't have the money for things like that. But when the friend mentioned that a wealthy real estate investor was also going to be there, the proverbial light bulb went off: Joe would, he decided, go on this trip so he could ask the wealthy investor what business he should be in, since clearly carpet cleaning wasn't working out.

While that man didn't give Joe the the sort of inspirational pep talk he'd been hoping for, he provided something far more useful when he asked Joe if there were people in Joe's line of work who *were* making money. Sure, Joe said, but those people had all sorts of resources he didn't. The man said, "If there are people who are successful in your business and you're not, the problem isn't your business—it's you."

What Joe needed to do, the man went on to explain, was learn fundamental business skills; otherwise he would just switch to another industry, spend between six months and two years learning the technical skills required and then end up repeating the same bad business habits that weren't working. Develop business skills that work, the man told him, and you'll have control over your life. Otherwise, you'll be chasing opportunities.

That's when Joe realized that he was 100 percent responsible for his success—or lack thereof.

And so he devoted himself to understanding marketing. This meant learning, reading, listening, stopping things that weren't working, and applying everything that he was learning to his business. That's when he realized that selling was all about getting someone intellectually and emotionally engaged and that marketing was all about storytelling (for a more thorough explanation of Joe's feelings about selling, Google "is selling evil?" and check out his video on the topic).

One of the first lessons Joe stumbled upon was Gary Halbert's advice to "can and clone yourself." So he hired a copywriter, using $1,800 he didn't have, to write *A Consumer's Guide to Carpet Cleaning*. He started mailing that report out, along with special offers, and also set up a pre-recorded phone message that people were instructed to listen to before hiring a carpet cleaner. In a six-month period, Joe went from making $2,300 per month to $12,300 per month.

His success only grew from there.

He now runs Genius Network and GeniusX, the highest-level marketing groups in the entire world (Genius Network costs $25,000 per year to join while GeniusX, which Joe runs with Dean Graziosi, costs $100,000). Almost all of Joe's clients are running multi-million-dollar companies.

Not bad for a guy who failed *Owning and Operating a Small Business* at Chandler-Gilbert Community College.

Anna's Confusion Over the Word "Creative"

Before Anna got sober, she had a succession of jobs writing for and editing magazines and websites. Although she had solid skills, she had a way of getting in her own way—or, more specifically, of getting in the boss' way. When she worked at *People* magazine, she'd always return from interviewing a celebrity and listen to her boss remind her of all the questions she'd probably forgotten to ask. Frustrated, overly sensitive and not understanding that he was only trying to help her, she'd tell him to stop picking on her. He'd react defensively, explaining that she shouldn't talk to him that way. The conversations would escalate, and he would tell her that if she continued to maintain that attitude, he'd have to fire her.

One day, he made good on that threat.

Anna always says she was fired for her addiction, but she doesn't mean that she was in the bathroom doing cocaine (that started happening a few jobs later). The truth, though, is that she was so insecure—and so scared of being found out that she was in over her head— that she reacted defensively to any criticism. And rather than admitting that she was intimidated by all the seasoned journalists in her midst, she masked her insecurity with bravado. Essentially, the same feelings that caused her to drink and use drugs to excess are the ones that got her fired.

Many other jobs followed, until Anna found herself trying to write screenplays, clinging to the idea that she would make it as a screen or TV writer. But her addiction had taken over by that point, and she became convinced that the only way she could "get the creative juices flowing" would be to do two lines of cocaine. Of course, those two "get started" lines would turn into four would turn into eight would turn into an all-nighter where she was really just shaking and re-writing the same few lines over and over again.

When she got sober, she suddenly learned how to deal with her feelings of insecurity and, perhaps as a result, she immediately landed her then-dream job: as a staff writer at (the now defunct) *Premiere* magazine, doing celebrity interviews as well as a column called *Party Girl* where she covered movie premieres and award shows. She went from that job to freelancing for magazines like *Details, Playboy, Cosmo* and *Redbook*, and that led to writing her first book, *Party Girl* (based on the idea of a former party girl getting a column called *Party Girl* just as she cleans up her act), and five more books after that.

To say the very least, dulling out our brains with depressants, stimulants, benzos and opiates—not to mention food, sex, gambling and other addictive substances and behaviors—causes great career limitations. Once we're able to move past that, we can build literally any career we want. We are resilient people, after all. We have fought for our lives—and won.

Why not put that fight toward getting the careers we want?

SECTION 2:
A Former Addict Makes an Amazing Employee

Want to hear something shocking that we both noticed when we cleaned up our respective acts? People in recovery are often the most intelligent, motivated, charming, resourceful and successful people around. If you're going to develop a difficult-to-maintain habit, after all, you're going to need to have certain skills—among them, intelligence, motivation, charm and resourcefulness.

Why the Workforce Needs More Recovering Addicts

Nowhere is the concept that former addicts make the best employees summarized better than in entrepreneur and *Forbes* columnist Tori Utley's TEDx Talk, *Why The Workforce Needs More Recovering Addicts* . She starts out the talk by saying that if you dropped a former addict and a non-addict off at the Canadian border, the person who wasn't addicted would get lost in the woods but the person who was addicted would make it home the same night for dinner.

In the talk, Utley—whose father is in recovery from addiction—discusses how she came to believe what she does about former addicts. She was working with two different groups of people—entrepreneurs and recovering addicts—when she started to notice something: the entrepreneurs were so risk-averse that they held themselves back, while the recovering addicts had more drive and hustle and overall moxie than any group of people she'd ever encountered.

Her point, ultimately, is that those in recovery from addiction know how to take small steps to tackle big problems because that's what they've had to do to survive. Utley also focuses on how honesty and hard work are two of the most crucial elements when it comes to successfully recovering from addiction.

Are there two more important qualities, she asks rhetorically, to look for in potential employees?

Utley and her father have created an organization called More Than an Addict, a non-profit whose purpose is to empower recovering addicts to pursue big dreams. While Anna encountered Utley when Utley profiled her for *Forbes*, Anna had been preaching the same message for years: at AfterPartyMagazine, the website she edited for three years with the help of a small staff, she tried to only hire addicts in recovery. While this originally started as a decision she came to because the bulk of the site's content focused on recovery, she noticed something whenever she veered away from her original determination and hired so-called normies: they weren't as good as the former addicts. They didn't work as hard, they weren't as determined to prove themselves and they ultimately didn't care as much.

Former addicts have passion—sometimes a little too much—but if that passion can be focused on success, there's literally nothing that can stop us.

SECTION 3:
Finding Your Passion

If you've been looking at life as a journey you're just meant to survive, it can be confusing at first to understand that you're now in a life where you can thrive. This is where the "life beyond your wildest dreams" that people in recovery talk about happens.

The problem is, it can be overwhelming to get into this state of mind.

But that's what we're asking you to do.

Could Sharing About Your Recovery Be Your Passion?

There are obviously many fields you can enter—we know people in recovery who are doctors, lawyers, agents, accountants, producers and everything else under the sun.

But many people we meet, like us, want to use what they've learned from overcoming addiction and make that into their career. Anna has a special name for these people—Light Hustlers—and through her company, aptly named Light Hustler, she helps them share their stories, through essays, articles, books and more.

Today, there's a whole universe of people out there talking and writing and sharing about those things we're not supposed to be talking about, in turn giving other people who may feel shame about these things permission to do the same.

It took Joe many years of struggling in shame to begin opening up. He eventually conquered his drug addiction but was struggling with sex addiction—often paying for escorts after leading high-level marketing groups, which kicked his shame into high gear. Eventually, he realized that he was going to need to come clean, so he started sharing openly about the way his trauma, and in particular the sexual abuse he'd suffered as a kid, had impacted his life. To his surprise, this didn't hurt his career in the slightest; in fact, since that point, some of the world's most successful and high-profile people who had been struggling with sex addiction in secret have come to Joe for help.

Anna was open about her recovery from addiction from the minute she entered recovery. She's always been a chronic over-sharer, someone who told a bartender, at three days of sobriety, that she wanted a Diet Coke because if she had anything stronger, she might be tempted to call her dealer.

Because Anna got sober in LA, where half the city is sober and arguably the other half needs to get sober, she didn't really know she wasn't supposed to be talking openly about addiction. She's also a Jew who's been in therapy since she was sixteen, so she was used to talking openly her issues by the time she entered recovery. Plus, she's a writer—that is, someone most people assume would be an addict. In short, she didn't know it was unusual to be sharing your recovery with the world until she was already out there doing it.

In the time since we've quit drugs, the world of recovery has blossomed. When we were seeking treatment, there was virtually no information out there at all about it—except for a few gossip magazine stories about where certain celebrities had gone to rehab. Now, addiction and recovery are mainstream issues, and there are hundreds, if not thousands, of bloggers, advocates and authors out there sharing their stories.

We now share a common goal: to help those who didn't grow up talking about their every feeling, who didn't bottom out in LA, who haven't had the experience of sharing their story and then having high-profile people reach out for help as a result, who may feel shame about their addictions or mental illness or the way they grew up or anything else under the sun—to share their dark, too.

Not everyone needs to shout it from the rooftops, of course. Though if they do, there's no telling how many people they can help.

A Light Hustler Out There: Attorney Lisa Smith

Some people who are sharing their addiction stories with the world aren't doing it as their main career but rather as side projects. One of those is attorney Lisa Smith (whose book, *Girl Walks Out of a Bar,* we recommended earlier and whose morning routine is detailed earlier in this book). As she told us, "Throughout my spiral into alcoholism and cocaine addiction, the reality of my life was a giant secret from everyone around me—my family, my friends and my co-workers."

After years of being a high-functioning attorney during the day and a cocaine-addicted alcoholic at night (which also fed into the day), she's discovered the ultimate freedom. "It is so liberating to be able to tell the truth and have the giant weight of both the addiction and the secrets lifted from my shoulders," she says. "I thought if I could share my story, it could help the next person be able to shed the giant weight they were carrying around and hopefully they could recover as well."

Like many people who have shared their story with the world, Smith has had the satisfaction of seeing the difference she has made in people's lives. "Not long after *Girl Walks Out of a Bar* came out, I got a message over Facebook from someone I didn't know telling me that after they read the book, they decided to go into treatment," she recalls. "It made me cry. I know what a scary, yet crucial, decision that can be, and I was beyond honored that my story could help in any way. That one message erased any doubts I might have had about the decision to go public."

Of course, Smith had her hesitations before busting out with her truth. "My biggest fear was that people in my professional and personal lives would judge me harshly, particularly if they viewed addiction as a weakness and not as the disease that I believe it is," she says. "When I decided to go public with my story, I also decided that I would not pull any punches. My book is raw and often ugly. But, in the end, it's hopeful."

Smith continues, "I have been blown away by how wrong I was about the reception I would receive. People don't even let me finish my story before they chime in with their own experiences and those of others in their lives. Everyone struggles. Everyone has stories we never would have guessed. But until we reach out and tell our truths, we have no idea what the next person is just waiting to talk about."

Someone Else Out There Sharing: Recovery Advocate Ryan Hampton

Ryan Hampton, whose miracle morning routine also appears in this book, has arguably made a bigger difference in more people's lives in a shorter amount of time than anyone we know.

The person *Forbes* magazine calls the "the recovering heroin addict shaking social media," Hampton watches most all of his articles for the *Huffington Post* and *The Hill* go viral. He's written a book for HarperCollins, is quoted in nearly every article about the recovery movement and is flown all over the world to share his opinions. And he's only been in recovery for a few years.

Hampton got started on this path after getting sober and then watching some of his closest friends die from overdoses. "I just kept thinking, 'In what world is it okay to not be outraged when dozens of your friends under the age of forty just fade away?'" he recalls. "It never sat right with me. And I just kept thinking to myself that maybe I needed to open up. Not just about addiction. But about who I was. I had ZERO idea what I was doing at first. Honestly, opening up about one thing led to another, and another, and another. Things and experiences such as my sexual identity, childhood trauma, and shit I never in a million years thought I'd be talking about just made their way to pen and paper. Stuff I'd locked away for decades just surfaced, and I finally felt comfortable accepting that it was part of my story."

Hampton is contacted by hundreds of people every week—those who are either trying to get sober, have gotten sober, or are watching loved ones succumb to or overcome addiction—but he's experienced something even more important than knowing that what he's doing makes a difference.

"The most valuable, unexpected benefit of this work is the ability to love myself no matter what," he says. "I've found purpose and value in what I do. My story doesn't scare me anymore. Through telling it, I've found freedom. And now I'm on a mission to re-create my experience in doing so for as many people as possible."

Of course, Hampton knows that not everyone is in a position where they can start telling the world their most private confessions. Still, he says, "I was so scared of being rejected before I opened up. I'd think, 'What if people laugh at me? What if people think this is stupid? What if I fail? What if people start pushing me away?' As it turns out, none of those fears were real. And to the few people who actually did think those things, I'm okay with it. Because for every one of those, I've gained meaningful connections with thousands more. I guess you can call that a fair trade."

Hampton's advice for those who are wondering whether or not they should come out about their addiction is fairly simple: "Embrace your story," he says. "Own it." Hampton had "no idea how many people out there shared the exact same experiences as I did. And it seemed as if they were just waiting for an invitation to share their own story, too. In a weird way, by telling your story, you give courage to others and invite them to do the same. We can shift cultural perceptions by owning our narratives and not allowing others to own them for us. My advice: do it. Tell your story. Drop the mic. And watch what happens. It's a pretty rad experience."

How Can You Discover Your Passion?

The best way to figure out what you want to do is to ask yourself. This may, of course, seem obvious, but the steps toward that conversation can be opaque. The process we recommend is to take a look at your skill set. Yes, you should examine what you love doing, but also think about some of the things you've done that have come remarkably easily or that people have looked to you for advice on. It can be something as unique as your ability to groom cats or as creative as your skill with language. Whatever it is, take note. If you don't know where to start—some of us have excelled for years at beating ourselves up, so noting our assets may not be standard practice—ask the people in your life for input.

Once you have a clearer idea of the direction you want to go, take out a journal or whiteboard and start brainstorming different ways you could go with that skill set. Writing talent, for example, can lead you to writing books or screenplays, but it can also allow you to write copy for marketing or advertising campaigns, teach or lead workshops. With entrepreneurial skills, you can start companies, become a consultant or do a myriad of other activities.

Of course, knowing where you can go isn't the same thing as going there. The best way to make sure you follow up is to get yourself an accountability partner or group. (For the high rollers, we highly recommend applying to Genius Network, of course; for those looking for something more basic, we suggest looking into Anna's Light Hustler Evolution accountability group.)

SECTION 4:
What the Worker in Recovery Needs to Remember

Something important to keep in mind, when it comes to jump-starting a career or re-entering one you were already engaged in but with a clearer head, is that people like us can sometimes overdo it. We also tend to have some habits that, when used appropriately, can be our best assets but, left unchecked, can get us into trouble.

How to Banish Perfectionism

Some of us feel like we need to make up for lost time. Others of us turned to substances or addictive behavior because we were afraid to face our imperfections. In other words, in recovery, we often try to seek perfection like it's required. If we're writers, this can mean rewriting and rewriting until the final text doesn't even say what we meant for it to say anymore. It can mean believing we have writer's block when really we're just waiting until the clouds metaphorically part open and we have the inspiration of a thousand people. If we're entrepreneurs, it can mean beating ourselves up if a launch or project doesn't have the earth-shattering success we'd been hoping for. During moments like this, it's important to keep in mind the popular recovery expression that "expectations are resentments under construction."

We all could stand to be reminded of the fact that no one's perfect, that we don't need to make up for the time we lost and that our struggles become our greatest lessons. Most of us could also surely stand to develop thicker skin. All those lessons that non-addicts were learning during our lost years—the heartbreak, the criticism, the rejection—we were blotting out. You could say that we were engaging in addictive behavior precisely to *avoid* those feelings.

There's a simple psychological explanation that describes sensitivity called the "orchid and the dandelion." Some kids are like dandelions, the theory goes. They can withstand criticism and difficult situations without being too impacted by any of it. Others are like orchids—sensitive to the extreme and needing just the right amount of light and temperature and water in order to feel okay. The dandelion and orchid theory can, in a basic way, explain why some incidents that register as traumatic for a certain kid won't affect another. It's safe to say that most people who develop addictive tendencies were—and remain—orchids.

In much the same way that Anna was overly sensitive when she worked at *People* magazine, reacting to criticism as if she were being punctured by arrows, she noticed when she was in the position to hire writers and then edit their work that the addicts in recovery were much more sensitive than the other writers. Addicts, even sober addicts, take things in and really feel them and while that can make us brilliant artists and compassionate people, it can also make us less-than-ideal employees. The best antidote for being overly reactive when we get our feelings hurt is to remind ourselves that nothing's personal and that no one's expecting us to be perfect.

If we can remember that the way we are is perfect already—that we, like everyone, are perfectly flawed—we can have miraculous lives. It all starts in the morning.

(All this being said, addiction—as we've mentioned—can play Whack-A-Mole, which is to say that once we've conquered one addiction, another one can pop up. If you have quit drugs but worry you're now behaving addictively about work, there are many tests out there that you can take.)

RECOVERY WARRIOR MORNING ROUTINE

JASON WAHLER
FACEBOOK.COM/JASONWAHLER
TWITTER: @WAHLERJASON
INSTAGRAM: @JASONWAHLER/

Jason Wahler is a host, actor and TV personality who appeared on hit shows like MTV'S *Laguna Beach* and *The Hills*. After years of publicly battling with addiction, he appeared on *Dr. Drew's Celebrity Rehab*. Jason has dedicated his life to raising awareness toward addiction and hopes to one day change the public's negative perception of this deadly disease. Currently, as the founder of Widespread Recovery and director of marketing for Tres Vistas Recovery, Jason's goal is to set the standard in aftercare starting with Southern California. On a regular basis, Jason works with various media outlets, celebrities, young adults, schools, law enforcement agencies, churches and athletes to promote addiction education and prevention. Jason also serves on the boards of the Los Angeles Mission and Rock to Recovery. He is on the honorary boards of the Prism Awards, Entertainment Industry Council, and the Brent Shapiro Foundation for Drug Awareness, along with serving as a writer and contributor to the *Huffington Post*.

Jason's morning routine:

- My daily routine has become a culmination of years of experience witnessing what works and what doesn't. Although every individual will have suggestions and advice, the beauty of humanity is our individuality. With that in mind, healthy habits and routines are all about creating patterns that work for you personally, but I would like to share my routine as I believe there may be someone out there it can apply to and help.

- One key to my morning routine is consistency. Consistency allows me to hold myself accountable for any shortcomings or procrastinations. By getting into a repeated routine, it's easy to determine where the wheels fell off the cart. Creating consistency and structure at the start of the day makes carrying that consistency and structure throughout the day much easier as well.

- The beginning of my day starts promptly at 6:00 a.m. So many people love their "snooze" button, but it's my mindfulness of the harmful effect of that button that gets me to rise and shine. Once I'm up, I like to collect my thoughts in a period of meditation. This gives me a sense of sanctuary to truly get my ducks lined up so that I can knock them down efficiently. It also helps me connect with myself and establish goals for the day. Without goals, a person is just "there" but not really doing anything.

- Once I've collected my thoughts and established my goals, I like to further reinforce my connection on a fellowship level by spending quality time with my family. Although I only spend about thirty minutes with my loving wife and our most recent addition—our beautiful baby girl, Delilah—I would like everyone to remember that life is about love, memories and the legacy you leave behind.

- Moving on from the spiritual side of my morning and transiting to the physical side, I find myself at the gym. Through working out and boxing specifically, I am able to complete my physical, mental and spiritual attunement as well as achieve the natural high from the workout itself. This is my first cup of coffee so to speak, as it gets my blood flowing and ready for the day ahead. After I'm done with my workout, I'm on a mission to find my real cup of coffee and a healthy breakfast to refuel, replenish and reinforce my well-being.

- Next on the agenda is a much-needed shower. The shower—with its running water—offers another soothing period of meditation for me to reflect on the progress of my morning thus far. This usually gets me pretty pumped to continue on to the next part of my morning.

- Where most people usually cringe getting ready for work, I love it. I relate this to a professional athlete in the sense that I'm in the locker room ready to make my plate appearance and smash one out of the park. My passion is helping people and getting dressed for work establishes a great sense of self-worth because I going to help people. On top of that, getting dressed and making sure everything is primped and proper reinforces my self-esteem as well. Feel good, look good, do good.

- Lastly, I am out the door, coffee in hand, on my way to do my day's duties. Although I set goals from the onset, I have periodic, routine self-evaluations because I strongly believe that if you're standing still, you can't move forward. While my routine works wonders for me and how I go about my day, I believe that this can apply to many people, especially the ones constantly trying to create more time in the day.

THE MIRACLE MORNING 30-DAY LIFE TRANSFORMATION CHALLENGE

*"An extraordinary life is all about daily,
continuous improvements in the areas that matter most."*
—ROBIN SHARMA

L et's play devil's advocate for a moment. Can *The Miracle Morning* really transform any area of your life or career in just thirty days? Can anything really make *that* significant of an impact, that quickly? Well, remember that it has already done this for thousands of others, and if it works for them, it can and will absolutely work for you.

Incorporating or changing any habit requires an acclimation period, so don't expect this to be effortless from day one. However, by making a commitment to yourself to stick with this, beginning each day with a Miracle Morning and leveraging the S.A.V.E.R.S. will quickly become the foundational habit that makes all others possible. Remember: *win the morning, and you set yourself up to win the day.*

The seemingly unbearable first few days of changing a habit are only temporary. While there's a lot of debate about how long it takes to implement a new habit, there is a powerful three-phase strategy that has proven successful for the hundreds of thousands of individuals who have learned how to conquer the snooze button and who now wake up every day for their Miracle Morning.

From Unbearable to Unstoppable:

The Three-Phase Strategy to Implement Any Habit in Thirty Days

As you take The Miracle Morning 30-Day Life Transformation Challenge, following is arguably the simplest and most effective strategy for implementing and sustaining any new habit in just thirty days. This will give you the mindset and approach you can take on as you build your new routine.

Phase One: Unbearable (Days One to Ten)

Phase One is when any new activity requires the most amount of conscious effort, and getting up early is no different. You're fighting existing habits, the very habits that have been entrenched in *who you are* for years.

In this phase, it's mind over matter—and if you don't mind, it'll definitely matter! The habits of hitting the snooze button and not making the most of your day are the same habits that hold you back from becoming the superstar recovery warrior you have always known you can be. So dig in and hold strong.

In Phase One, while you battle existing patterns and limiting beliefs, you'll find out what you're made of and what you're capable of. You need to keep pushing, stay committed to your vision, and hang in there. Trust us when we say you can do this!

We know it can be daunting on day five to realize you still have twenty-five days to go before your transformation is complete and you've become a bona fide morning person. Keep in mind that on day five, you're more than halfway through the first phase and well on your way. Remember: your initial feelings are not going to last forever. In fact, you owe it to yourself to persevere because, in no time at all, you'll be getting the exact results you want as you become the person you've always wanted to be!

Phase Two: Uncomfortable (Days Eleven to Twenty)

In Phase Two, your body and mind begin to acclimate to waking up earlier. You'll notice that getting up starts to get a tiny bit easier, but it's not yet a habit; it's not quite who you are and likely won't feel natural yet.

The biggest temptation at this level is to reward yourself by taking a break, especially on the weekends. A question posted quite often in the Miracle Morning Community is, "How many days a week do you get up early for your Miracle Morning?" Our answer—and the one that's most common from longtime Miracle Morning practitioners— is *every single day*.

Once you've made it through Phase One, you're past the hardest period. So keep going! Why on earth would you want to go through that first phase again by taking one or two days off? Trust me, you wouldn't, so don't!

Phase Three: Unstoppable (Days Twenty-One to Thirty)

Early rising is now not only a habit, it has literally become part of *who you are*, part of your identity. Your body and mind will have become accustomed to your new way of being. These next ten days are important for cementing the habit in yourself and your life.

As you engage in the Miracle Morning practice, you will also develop an appreciation for the three distinct phases of habit change. A side benefit is you will realize you can identify, develop, and adopt any habit that serves you—including the habits of exceptional people in recovery that we have included in this book.

Now that you've learned the simplest and most effective strategy for successfully implementing and sustaining any new habit in thirty days, you know the mindset and approach that you need to complete

The Miracle Morning 30-Day Transformation Challenge. All that's required is for you to commit to getting started and following through.

Consider the Rewards

When you commit to The Miracle Morning 30-Day Transformation Challenge, you will be building a foundation for success in every area of your life, for the rest of your life. By waking up each morning and practicing the Miracle Morning, you will begin each day with extraordinary levels of *discipline* (the crucial ability to get yourself to follow through with your commitments), *clarity* (the power you'll generate from focusing on what's most important), and *personal development* (perhaps the single most significant determining factor in your success). Thus, in the next thirty days you'll find yourself quickly *becoming the person* you need to be to create the extraordinary levels of personal, professional, and financial success you truly desire.

You'll also be transforming the Miracle Morning from a concept that you may be excited (and possibly a little nervous) to "try" into a lifelong habit, one that will continue to develop you into the person you need to be to create the life you've always wanted. You'll begin to fulfill your potential and see results in your life far beyond what you've ever experienced before.

In addition to developing successful habits, you'll also be developing the *mindset* you need to improve your life—both internally and externally. By practicing the Life S.A.V.E.R.S. each day, you'll be experiencing the physical, intellectual, emotional, and spiritual benefits of **S**ilence, **A**ffirmations, **V**isualization, **E**xercise, **R**eading, and **S**cribing. You'll immediately feel less stressed, more centered, more focused, happier and more excited about your life. You'll be generating more energy, clarity and motivation to move toward your highest goals and dreams (especially those you've been putting off far too long).

Remember, your life situation will improve after—but only *after*—you develop yourself into the person you need to be to improve it. That's exactly what these next thirty days of your life can be—a new beginning, and a new you.

You Can Do This!

If you're feeling nervous, hesitant, or concerned about whether or not you will be able to follow through with this for thirty days, relax—it's completely normal to feel this way. This is especially true if waking up in the morning is something you've found challenging in the past. It's not only expected that you would be a bit hesitant or nervous, but it's actually a very good sign! It's a sign that you're *ready* to commit; otherwise, you wouldn't be nervous.

Ready? Here we go…

Four Steps to Begin the Miracle Morning (30-Day) Transformation Challenge

Step 1: Get The Miracle Morning 30-Day Transformation Challenge Fast Start Kit

Visit www.TMMBook.com to download your free Miracle Morning 30-Day Life Transformation Challenge Fast Start Kit— complete with the exercises, affirmations, daily checklists, tracking sheets, and everything else you need to make starting and completing The Miracle Morning 30-Day Life Transformation Challenge as easy as possible. Please take a minute to do this now.

Step 2: Plan Your First Miracle Morning for Tomorrow

If you haven't already began, commit to (and schedule) your first Miracle Morning as soon as possible—ideally *tomorrow*. Yes, actually write it into your schedule and decide where it will take place. Remember, it's recommended that you leave your bedroom and remove yourself from the temptation of your bed altogether. My Miracle Morning takes place every day on my living room couch while everyone else in my house is still sound asleep. I've heard from people who do their Miracle Morning sitting outside in nature, such as on their porch or deck, or at a nearby park. Do yours where you feel most comfortable, but also where you won't be interrupted.

Step 3: Read Page One of the Fast Start Kit and Do the Exercises

Read the introduction in your Miracle Morning 30-Day Life Transformation Challenge Fast Start Kit, then please follow the instructions and complete the exercises. Like anything in life that's worthwhile, successfully completing The Miracle Morning 30-Day Life Transformation Challenge requires a bit of preparation. It's important that you do the initial exercises in your Fast Start Kit (which shouldn't take you more than an hour) and keep in mind that your Miracle Morning will always start with the *preparation* you do the day or night before to get yourself ready mentally, emotionally, and logistically for your Miracle Morning. This preparation includes following the steps in chapter 5: The Five-Step Snooze-Proof Wake-Up Strategy.

Step 3.1: Get an Accountability Partner (Recommended)

The overwhelming evidence for the correlation between success and accountability is undeniable. While most people resist being held accountable, it is hugely beneficial to have someone who will hold us to higher standards than we'll hold ourselves to. All of us can benefit from the support of an accountability partner, so it's highly recommended—but definitely not required—that you reach out to someone in your circle of influence (family member, friend, colleague, significant other, etc.) and invite them to join you in The Miracle Morning 30-Day Life Transformation Challenge.

Not only does having someone to hold us accountable increase the odds that we will follow through, but joining forces with someone else is simply more fun! Consider that when you're excited about something and committed to doing it on your own, there is a certain level of power in that excitement and in your individual commitment. However, when you have someone else in your life—a friend, family member, or co-worker—who's as excited about and committed to it as you are, it's much more powerful.

Call, text, or email one or more people today, and invite them to join you for The Miracle Morning 30-Day Life Transformation Challenge. The quickest way to get them up to speed is to send them the link to www.MiracleMorning.com so they can get free and immediate access to The Miracle Morning Fast Start Kit, including:

- **The FREE Miracle Morning video training**
- **The FREE Miracle Morning audio training**
- **Two FREE Chapters of *The Miracle Morning* book**

It will cost them nothing, and you'll be teaming up with someone who is also committed to taking their life to the next level so the two of you can offer support, encouragement, and accountability to one another.

IMPORTANT: Don't wait until you have an accountability partner on board to do your first Miracle Morning and start The 30-Day Life Transformation Challenge. Whether or not you've found someone to embark on the journey with you, we still recommend scheduling and doing your first Miracle Morning tomorrow—no matter what. Don't wait. You'll be even more capable of inspiring someone else to do the Miracle Morning with you if you've already experienced a few days of it. Get started. Then, as soon as you can, invite a friend, family member, or co-worker to visit www.MiracleMorning.com to get their free Miracle Morning Fast Start Kit.

In less than an hour, they'll be fully capable of being your Miracle Morning accountability partner—and probably a little inspired as well.

Are You Ready to Take *Your* Life to the Next Level?

What is the next level in your personal or professional life? Which areas need to be transformed in order for you to reach that level? Give yourself the gift of investing just thirty days to make significant improvements in your life, one day at a time. No matter what your past has been, you *can* change your future by changing the present.

RECOVERY WARRIOR MORNING ROUTINE

PETER MARSTON JR.

FACEBOOK.COM/PETERMARSTONJR

LINKEDIN: PETERMARSTONJR

INSTAGRAM: @REBOSPETE25

Peter is a person in long-term recovery who is a husband, father, entrepreneur, real estate investor, speaker, and addiction recovery expert. He speaks frequently about addiction, personal growth and development, sharing his story with others in the hope of inspiring people to live their best lives in recovery. Sobriety has allowed Peter to pursue his entrepreneurial dreams and live his purpose creating opportunities and helping others. He owns a growing HVAC company based in New Hampshire and has invested in real estate for the last several years, acquiring multiple rental properties. Peter is also a partner at Bonfire Behavioral Health, which strives to foster the growth and confidence of its clients using a proven, solution-based model of recovery while drawing from a rich variety of support sources.

Peter's miracle morning:

- My Miracle Morning routine has been a keystone habit for me, implemented many years ago after countless failed attempts at sobriety. It wasn't until I started practicing the Miracle Morning routine in early recovery (at age twenty-five) that I finally found peace, contentment and joy. I got sober after a failed suicide attempt on May 10, 2008. My journey of sobriety began on Mother's Day: May 11, 2008.

- I can't emphasize enough the importance of a morning routine in early sobriety. In the context of being a business owner and entrepreneur, the Miracle Morning has been critical to my growth as a leader, husband, father and business owner. My morning routine has evolved over the last few years.

- In the beginning of my sobriety, my routine looked like this: I woke up, hit my knees and prayed. (I never prayed before getting sober, unless it was in the back of a police car praying for the big guy to get me out of a bad situation.) After praying, I would write. I would write about anything and everything. I wrote about my feelings, my experiences being newly sober, sayings I would hear in meetings, my relationships. After my journal entry, I would write down several positive affirmations, and then I would read them out loud in the mirror. This literally changed the way I viewed myself as a person. I started to develop confidence, grow my self-esteem and improve my mindset through the power of positive affirmations. After the affirmations, I would read books. I read every single day in early recovery. The books I read were deep, impactful and spiritual in nature. I was feeding my brain positive content, and this was completely foreign to me. I also wrote down goals. For the first time in my life, I realized that I had the potential to live a better life and not be a slave to drugs and alcohol. The goals I set in early recovery all were manifested through focus and discipline. I also started working out three times a week and became very committed to being the best version of myself. These new habits in early recovery changed my life. My morning routine has continued to develop and deepen since the early days of my recovery. I do it because it worked then, and it still works today. It allows me to continuously improve, help others and stay focused on what I believe being an entrepreneur is all about—creating opportunities for myself, my family and others.

- The Miracle Morning continues to provide a framework that was not available to me when I first got into recovery. There's structure and routine, which I pour energy and effort into on a daily basis. The Miracle Morning has been the greatest game-changer for my recovery, which has intrinsically affected every other area of my life.

— CONCLUSION —

LET TODAY BE THE DAY YOU GIVE UP WHO YOU'VE BEEN FOR WHO YOU CAN BECOME

"Every day, think as you wake up, 'Today I am fortunate
to have woken up, I am alive, I have a precious human life,
I am not going to waste it. I am going to use all my energies
to develop myself, to expand my heart out to others. I am
going to benefit others as much as I can.'"
—DALAI LAMA

"Things do not change. We change."
—HENRY DAVID THOREAU

Where you are is a result of who you *were*, but where you go from here depends entirely on who you choose to be, from this moment forward.

Now is your time. Decide that today is the most important day of your life, because it is who you are becoming now—based on the choices that you make and the actions that you take—that will determine who and where you are going to be for the rest of your life. Don't put off creating and experiencing the life—happiness, health, wealth, success, and love—that you truly want and deserve.

As one of Hal's mentors, Kevin Bracy, always urged: "Don't wait to be great." If you want your life to improve, you have to improve yourself first. You can download The Miracle Morning 30-Day Life Transformation Fast Start Kit at www.TMMBook.com. Then, with or without an accountability partner, commit to completing your 30-day challenge so that you will immediately begin accessing more of your potential than you ever have before. Imagine…just one month from now, you will be well on your way to transforming every area of your life.

Let's Keep Helping Others

May we ask you a quick favor?

If this book has added value to your life, if you feel like you're better off after reading it, and you see that the Miracle Morning can be a new beginning for you to take any—or every—area of your life to the next level, we're hoping you'll do something for someone you care about: give this book to them. Let them borrow your copy.

Ask them to read it so that they have the opportunity to transform their life for the better. Or, if you're not willing to give up your copy quite yet because you're planning on going back and re-reading it, maybe you get them their own copy. It could be for no special occasion at all, other than to say, "Hey, I love and appreciate you, and I want to help you live your best life. Read this."

If you believe, as we do, that being a great friend (or family member) is about helping your friends and loved ones to become the best versions of themselves, we encourage you to share this book with them.

Together, we are truly elevating the consciousness of humanity, one morning at a time.

Thank you so much.

RECOVERY WARRIOR MIRACLE MORNING ROUTINE

JESSE HARLESS
FACEBOOK.COM/JESSEHARLESS22
TWITTER: @JESSEHARLESS22
INSTAGRAM: @JESSEHARLESS221

Jesse's journey of recovery began in 2005 when he was faced with multiple felony charges for his addiction to painkillers. He's a facilitator, speaker, coach, and mentor for people in recovery, as well as the founder of Entrepreneurs in Recovery. Jesse graduated from Rivier University with his Master's in Mental Health Counseling.

Jesse's morning routine:

- The first thing I do when I wake up is drink between six to eight ounces of water, followed by consuming my plant-based multivitamin, which I put next to my water the night before so I won't forget. I brush my teeth and throw cold water on my face. I'm now ready to dive into the Miracle Morning S.A.V.E.R.S. routine.

- My living room couch is my meditation spot. I use the Insight Timer app to track the length of my meditations. My meditation consists of twenty minutes of the "See Hear Feel" technique I learned from Julianna Raye, the founder of Unified Mindfulness.

- During my last five minutes of meditation, I do two visualizations. My first visualization is seeing myself easily accomplishing each task for the day. My second visualization is me accomplishing my most important goal for the quarter or the year. This second visualization provides feelings of joy and gratitude.

- Next, I use the Five Minute Journal app to list three things I'm grateful for, three things I will do to make my day great, and a daily affirmation. I use my Kindle app to do my reading for the next five to ten minutes. I prefer reading books that provide valuable tools, thoughts, or ideas I can put into practice for the day.

- My exercise comes in the form of five minutes of simple yoga stretches. I can barely touch my toes, but yoga makes me feel great. I follow this with affirmations I have written on index cards. I read each affirmation to myself out loud. My morning routine always finishes with a cold shower.

- The Life S.A.V.E.R.S have been a game-changer for my recovery and my career. I have continued my Miracle Morning routine for the last two-and-a-half years straight. Taking time for myself every morning has empowered me to create the life I want. There are days when I miss a part of my morning routine, and guess what, it still works! Every morning, I have an abundance of energy and mental clarity to achieve my goals.

A SPECIAL INVITATION FROM HAL

Readers and practitioners of *The Miracle Morning* have co-created an extraordinary community consisting of over 200,000 like-minded individuals from around the world who wake up each day *with purpose* and dedicate time to fulfilling the unlimited potential that is within all of us, while helping others to do the same.

As author of *The Miracle Morning*, I felt that I had a responsibility to create an online community where readers could come together to connect, get encouragement, share best practices, support one another, discuss the book, post videos, find an accountability partner, and even swap smoothie recipes and exercise routines.

However, I honestly had no idea that The Miracle Morning Community would become one of the most positive, engaged, and supportive online communities in the world, but it has. I'm constantly astounded by the caliber and the character of our members, which presently includes people from over seventy countries and is growing daily.

Just go to **www.MyTMMCommunity.com** and request to join The Miracle Morning Community on Facebook. You'll immediately be able to connect with 130,000+ people who are already practicing TMM. While you'll find many who are just beginning their Miracle Morning journey, you'll find even more who have been at it for years and will happily share advice, support, and guidance to accelerate your success.

I moderate the Community and check in regularly, so I look forward to seeing you there! If you'd like to connect with me personally on social media, just follow **@HalElrod** on Twitter and **Facebook. com/YoPalHal** on Facebook. Let's connect soon!

— BONUS CHAPTER —

THE MIRACLE EQUATION

By Hal Elrod

"There are only two ways to live your life.
One is though nothing is a miracle.
The other is though everything is a miracle."

—ALBERT EINSTEIN

You understand now that you *can* wake up early, maintain extraordinary levels of energy, direct your focus, and master the not-so-obvious recovery skills from Anna David and Joe Polish. If you also apply what follows to every aspect of your life, you're going to go much further; you're going to make your life truly exceptional.

To make this leap, there is one more helpful tool for you to add to your toolbox, and it's called The Miracle Equation.

The Miracle Equation is the underlying strategy that I used to realize my full potential as a salesperson and as a friend, spouse, and parent. And it has to do with how you handle your goals. One of my mentors, Dan Casetta, taught me: "The purpose of a goal isn't to hit the goal. The real purpose is to develop yourself into the type of person who can achieve your goals, regardless of whether you hit that particular one or not. It is who you become by giving it everything you have until the last moment—regardless of your results—that matters most."

When you make the decision to stick with a seemingly unachievable goal, despite the fact that the possibility of failure is high, you will become especially focused, faithful, and intentional. When your objective is truly ambitious, it will require you to find out what you are really made of!

Two Decisions

As with any great challenge, you need to make decisions related to achieving the goal. You can set a deadline and then create your own agenda by asking yourself, "If I were to achieve my goal on the deadline, what decisions would I have to make and commit to in advance?"

And you'll find that whatever the goal, the two decisions that would make the biggest impact are *always the same.* They form the basis for The Miracle Equation.

The First Decision: Unwavering Faith

There was a time in my life when I was trying to achieve an impossible sales goal. I'll use that as an example to show you what I mean. Though this comes from my sales experience, I'll show you how it applies within the context of addiction recovery (or any context, really). It was a stressful time and I was already facing fear and self-doubt, but my thought process about the goal forced me to an important realization: to achieve the seemingly impossible, I would have to maintain unwavering faith every day, *regardless of my results.*

I knew that there would be moments when I would doubt myself and times when I would be so far off track that the goal would no longer seem achievable. But it would be those moments when I would have to override self-doubt with unshakeable faith.

To keep that level of faith in those challenging moments, I repeated what I call my Miracle Mantra:

I will _____ (reach my goal), no matter what. There is no other option.

Understand that maintaining unwavering faith isn't *normal*. It's not what most people do. When it doesn't look like the desired result is likely, average performers give up the faith that it's possible. When the game is on the line, a team is down on the scorecards, and there are only seconds left, it is only the top performers—the Michael Jordans of the world—who, without hesitation, tell their team, "Give me the ball."

The rest of the team breathes a sigh of relief because they're freed from their fear of missing the game-winning shot, while Michael Jordan is backed by a decision he made at some point in his life that he would maintain unwavering faith, despite the fact that he might miss. (And although Michael Jordan missed twenty-six game-winning shots in his career, his faith that he would make every single one never wavered.)

That's the first decision that very successful people make, and it's yours for the making, too.

When you're working toward a goal and you're not on track, what is the first thing that goes out the window? *The faith that the outcome you want is possible.* Your self-talk turns negative: *I'm not on track. It doesn't look like I'm going to reach my goal.* And with each passing moment, your faith decreases.

You don't have to settle for that. You have the ability and the choice to maintain that same unwavering faith, no matter what, and regardless of the results. This is key in addiction recovery because results are often out of your direct control. You may doubt yourself or have a bad day. In the darkest moments, you wonder if everything will turn out okay. But you must find—over and over again—your faith that all things are possible and hold it throughout your journey.

It's very important that you see your role as a recovering addict as directly related to other high-achieving professions, because the parallels are unmistakable. If you don't take time to see the parallels here, you may find that you focus on the failures of your recovery instead of the successes. And if you focus on the failures, others around you will too, and that's not what you want. So stay with me.

Elite athletes maintain unwavering faith that they can make every shot they take. That faith—and the faith you need to develop—isn't based on probability. It comes from a whole different place. Most salespeople operate based on what is known as the *law of averages*. But what we're talking about here is the *law of miracles*. When you miss shot after shot, you have to tell yourself what Michael Jordan tells himself: *I've missed three, but I want the ball next, and I'm going to make that next shot.*

And if you miss that one, *your faith doesn't waver.* You repeat the Miracle Mantra to yourself:

I will _____ (reach my goal), no matter what. There is no other option.

Then, you simply uphold your integrity and do what it is that you say you are going to do.

An elite athlete may be having the worst game ever, where it seems like in the first three quarters of the game, they can't make a shot to save their life. Yet in the fourth quarter, right when the team needs them, they start making those shots. They always want the ball; they always have belief and faith in themselves. In the fourth quarter, they score three times as many shots as they made in the first three quarters of the game.

Why? They have conditioned themselves to have unwavering faith in their talents, skills, and abilities, regardless of what it says on the scoreboard or their stats sheet.

They also combine their unwavering faith with part two of The Miracle Equation: extraordinary effort.

The Second Decision: Extraordinary Effort

When you allow your faith to go out the window, effort almost always follows right behind it. *After all,* you tell yourself, *what's the point in even trying to achieve your goal if it's not possible?* Suddenly, you find yourself wondering how you're ever going to wake up early for your Miracle Morning each day, let alone reach the big goal you've been working toward.

I've been there many times, feeling deflated, thinking, *What's the point of even trying?* And you might easily think, *There's no way I can make it. My life is headed in the wrong direction.*

That's where extraordinary effort comes into play. You need to stay focused on your original goal, to connect to the vision you had for it, that big *why* in your heart and mind when you set the goal in the first place.

Like me, you need to reverse engineer the goal. Ask yourself, *If I'm at the end of this month and this goal were to have happened, what would I have done? What would I have needed to do?*

Whatever the answer, you will need to stay consistent and persevere, regardless of your results. You have to believe you can still ring the bell of success at the end. You have to maintain unwavering faith and extraordinary effort—until the buzzer sounds. That's the only way that you create an opportunity for the miracle to happen.

If you do what the average person does—what our built-in human nature tells us to do—you'll be just like every other average recovering addict. Don't choose to be that average person! Remember: your thoughts and actions create your results and are therefore a self-fulfilling prophecy. Manage them wisely.

Allow me to introduce you to your edge—the strategy that will practically ensure every one of your goals is realized.

The Miracle Equation

Unwavering Faith + Extraordinary Effort = Miracles

It's easier than you think. The secret to maintaining unwavering faith is to recognize that it's a mindset and a *strategy*—it's not concrete. In fact, it's elusive. You can never make *every* sale. No athlete makes *every* shot. You can never win every battle. So, you have to program yourself automatically to have the unwavering faith to drive you to keep putting forth the extraordinary effort—regardless of the results.

Remember, the key to putting this equation into practice, to maintaining unwavering faith in the midst of self-doubt, is the Miracle Mantra:

I will _____, no matter what. There is no other option.

Once you set a goal, put that goal into the Miracle Mantra format. Yes, you're going to say your affirmations every morning (and maybe every evening, too). But all day, every day, you're going to repeat your Miracle Mantra to yourself. As you're driving the kids to school or taking the train to the office, while you're on the treadmill, in the shower, in line at the grocery store—in other words: *everywhere you go.*

Your Miracle Mantra will fortify your faith and be the self-talk you need to make just one more attempt, try after try.

Bonus Lesson

Remember what I learned from my mentor Dan Casetta on the purpose of goals. You have to become the type of person who *can* achieve the goal. You won't always reach the goal, but you can become someone who maintains unwavering faith and puts forth extraordinary effort, regardless of your results. That's how you become the type of person you need to become to achieve extraordinary goals consistently.

And while reaching the goal almost doesn't matter (almost!), more often than not, you'll reach your goal. Do elite athletes win every time? No. But they win most of the time. And you'll win most of the time, too.

At the end of the day, you can wake up earlier, do the Life S.A.V.E.R.S. with passion and excitement; get organized, focused, and intentional; and master every challenge like a champ. And yet, if you don't combine unwavering faith with extraordinary effort, you won't reach the levels of success you seek.

The Miracle Equation gives you access to forces outside of anyone's understanding, using an energy that I might call God, the Universe, the Law of Attraction, or even good luck. I don't know how it works; I just know that it works.

You've read this far—you clearly want success more than almost anything. Commit to following through with every aspect, including The Miracle Equation. You deserve it, and I want you to have it!

Putting It into Action:

1. Write out the Miracle Equation and put it where you will see it every day: **Unwavering Faith + Extraordinary Effort = Miracles (UF + EE = M∞)**

2. Decide your number one goal for your recovery journey this year. What goal, if you were to accomplish it, would bring you closest to your ideal life?

3. Write your Miracle Mantra: *I will _____ (insert your goals and daily actions here), no matter what. There is no other option.*

It is more about who you become in the process. You'll expand your self-confidence and, regardless of your results, the very next time you attempt to reach a goal, and every time after that, you'll be the type of person who gives it all they've got.

Closing Remarks

Congratulations! You have done what only a small percentage of people do: read an entire book. If you've come this far, that tells me something about you: you have a thirst for more. You want to become more, do more, contribute more, and earn more.

Right now, you have the unprecedented opportunity to infuse the Life S.A.V.E.R.S. into your daily life and business, upgrade your daily routine, and ultimately upgrade your *life* to a first-class experience beyond your wildest dreams. Before you know it, you will be reaping the astronomical benefits of the habits that top achievers use daily.

Five years from now, your family life, business, relationships, and income will be a direct result of one thing: *who you've become*. It's up to you to wake up each day and dedicate time to becoming the best version of yourself. Seize this moment in time, define a vision for your future, and use what you've learned in this book to turn your vision into your reality.

Imagine a time just a few years from now when you come across the journal you started after completing this book. In it, you find the goals you wrote down for yourself—dreams you didn't dare speak out loud at the time. And as you look around, you realize *your dreams now represent the life you are living.*

Right now, you stand at the foot of a mountain you can easily and effortlessly climb. All you need to do is continue waking up each day for your Miracle Morning and use the Life S.A.V.E.R.S. day after day, month after month, year after year, as you continue to take your *self*, your *family*, and your *success* to levels beyond what you've ever experienced before.

Combine your Miracle Morning with a commitment to master your recovery principles and use The Miracle Equation to create results that most people only dream of.

This book was written as an expression of what we know will work for you, to take every area of your life to the next level, faster than you may currently believe is possible. Miraculous performers weren't born that way—they have simply dedicated their lives to developing themselves and their skills to achieve everything they've ever wanted.

You can become one of them, I promise.

Taking Action: The 30-Day Miracle Morning Challenge

Now it is time to join the tens of thousands of people who have transformed their lives with the Miracle Morning. Join the community online at TMMBook.com and download the toolkit to get you started *today*.

ABOUT THE AUTHORS

HAL ELROD is on a mission to *Elevate the Consciousness of Humanity, One Morning at a Time.* As one of the highest rated keynote speakers in the America, creator of one of the fastest growing and most engaged online communities in existence and author of one of the highest rated books in the world, ***The Miracle Morning***—which has been translated into 27 languages, has over 2,000 five-star Amazon reviews and is practiced daily by over 500,000 people in 70+ countries—he is doing exactly that.

The seed for Hal's life's work was planted at age twenty, when Hal was found dead at the scene of a horrific car accident. Hit head-on by a drunk driver at seventy miles per hour, he broke eleven bones, died for six minutes, and suffered permanent brain damage. After six days in a coma, he woke to face his unimaginable reality—which included being told by doctors that he would never walk again.

Defying the logic of doctors and proving that all of us can overcome even seemingly insurmountable adversity to achieve anything we set our minds to, Hal went on to not only walk but to run a 52-mile ultramarathon and become a hall of fame business achiever—all before the age of 30.

Then, in November of 2016, Hal nearly died again. With his kidneys, lungs, and heart of the verge of failing, he was diagnosed with a very rare, very aggressive form of leukemia and given a 30% chance of living. After enduring the most difficult year of his life, Hal is now cancer-free and furthering his mission as the Executive Producer of ***The Miracle Morning Movie***.

Most importantly, Hal is beyond grateful to be sharing his life with the woman of his dreams, Ursula Elrod, and their two children in Austin, Texas.

For more information on Hal's keynote speaking, live events, books, the movie and more, visit www.HalElrod.com.

ANNA DAVID is the *New York Times*-bestselling author of two novels and four non-fiction books about addiction, recovery and relationships. She's been published in *The New York Times, Time, The LA Times, Vanity Fair, Playboy, Vice* and *Women's Health*, among many others; written about in numerous publications including *Forbes, Martha Stewart Living, Entrepreneur* and *Allure*; and has appeared repeatedly on *The Today Show, Hannity, Attack of the Show, Dr. Drew, Red Eye, The Talk* and numerous other programs on Fox News, NBC, CBS, MTV, VH1 and E News. She is the CEO of Light Hustler, a company that helps people share their dark to find their light, through online coaching programs, writing courses, workshops, a storytelling show, a podcast and more. She speaks at colleges across the country about relationships, addiction and recovery.. You can find out more about her at AnnaDavid.com.

JOE POLISH is the founder of Genius Network® and GeniusX®; president of Piranha Marketing Inc.; co-founder of 10XTalk.com and ILoveMarketing.com; and creator of the *Genius Network®, Genius Recovery* podcasts along with co-creator of the *10x Talk* and *I Love Marketing* podcasts, four highly popular free podcasts on iTunes. Joe's marketing expertise has been utilized to build thousands of businesses and has generated hundreds of millions of dollars for his clients, ranging from large corporations to small family-owned businesses. Known for his entrepreneurial focus on value creation, connection, and contribution, Joe's leadership is the reason he's one of the most sought-after marketers alive today. Joe has helped raised over $3 million for Virgin Unite, Sir Richard Branson's foundation. His current philanthropic endeavors include JoeVolunteer.com, ArtistsForAddicts.com and Genius Recovery. Joe's mission is to help change the global conversation surrounding addiction and addicts from one of judgement to one of compassion.

HONORÉE CORDER is the author of dozens of books, including *You Must Write a Book, The Prosperous Writers* book series, *Like a Boss* book series, *Vision to Reality, Business Dating, The Successful Single Mom* book series, *If Divorce is a Game, These are the Rules,* and *The Divorced Phoenix*. She is also Hal Elrod's business partner in *The Miracle Morning* book series. Honorée coaches business professionals, writers, and aspiring non-fiction authors who want to publish their books to bestseller status, create a platform, and develop multiple streams of income. She also does all sorts of other magical things, and her badassery is legendary. You can find out more at HonoreeCorder.com.

Want to read Anna's first book about addiction?

"With Party Girl, Anna David
has invented what could be a
new subgenre: Chick Lit with a
Message"

New York Post

"A recovery story disguised as a
dishy, dirty beach read"

Huffington Post

You can!

Acidly hilarious and achingly honest, **Party Girl** is a harrowing ride through the world of Hollywood excess with a heroine who's deliciously flawed. Whether snorting coke or crying in rehab, hooking up or breaking down, Amelia Stone makes her way across the treacherous grounds of addiction, self-destruction, and recovery without ever losing her sharp wit, unapologetic candor, or odds-defying optimism.

Wondering if you should share your story of recovery?

Photo: Christopher Medak

Go to
lighthustler.com/quiz
to find out.

⟳ **GENIUS** RECOVERY

www.GeniusRecovery.com is the BEST place in the world to find interviews with RECOVERY EXPERTS.

OUR MISSION is to change the global conversation about how people view and treat addicts, with COMPASSION instead of judgement, and to help find the best forms of treatment that have EFFICACY, and SHARE those with the world.

VISIT GeniusRecovery.com for exclusive interviews with experts to educate, and inspire happiness, health, serenity, and sobriety.

EXPLORE our comprehensive resource center, curated for you with access to the very best blogs, websites, apps, and organizations for recovery.

Joe Polish

The Opposite of Addiction is CONNECTION.

Connect with Community Now at www.GeniusRecovery.com and ❶ www.Facebook.com/Groups/GeniusRecovery

ARTISTS FOR ADDICTS

VISION: Art as a Force for Good

Aiming to change the global conversation from one of judgement to compassion.

Every year, more addicts suffer at the hands of a system that punishes victims of addiction, and fails to provide treatments that break the cycle. A group that suffers greatly from addiction are artists, who often share a sensitivity to life that makes them more vulnerable.

Joe Polish came up with the idea for Artists For Addicts when he realized that artists and the arts may have many of the answers for this crisis. Artists For Addicts is a platform for stories and art, and a safe place to explore this difficult subject in creative ways. If YOU appreciate art as a force for good, or you are someone who has used the power of art to heal from addiction, stay in recovery, or support a loved one, you belong here, and we would love to hear from you.

Get Involved: www.ArtistsForAddicts.com
Follow & Share: www.Facebook.com/ArtistsForAddicts

Watch our first documentary film "Black Star"

WINNER
Audience Award
Best Short Film
ILLUMINATE
Film Festival
2018

Artists for Addict's first film, Black Star, documenting the creation of the first AFA art by artist Jon Butcher, was the Audience Award WINNER at its World Premiere in the 2018 Illuminate Film Festival. (Akira Chan, Blackstar Director and AFA Partner, left. Joe Polish, AFA Founder & Black Star Producer, right.) Access the film and art at www.ArtistsForAddicts.com

THE MIRACLE MORNING SERIES

The Journal

for Salespeople

for Real Estate Agents

for Network Marketers

for Writers

for Entrepreneurs

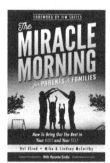

for Parents & Families

for College Students

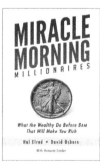

Millionaires

COMPANION GUIDES & WORKBOOKS

Art of Affirmations

**for Network Marketers
90-Day Action Plan**

Companion Planner

**for Salespeople
Companion Guide**

**for College Students
Companion Planner**

THE **MIRACLE MORNING** SERIES
Best Selling Author **HAL ELROD**

BOOK HAL to SPEAK

"Bringing Hal in to be the Keynote speaker at our annual conference was the best investment we could have made. –**Fidelity National Title**

"Hal was the featured Keynote speaker for 400 of our TOP Sales performers and executive team. He gave us a plan that was so simple, we had no choice but to put it in action immediately."
–**Art Van Furniture**

"Hal received 9.8 our of 10 from our members. That never happens." –**Entrepreneur Organization (NYC Chapter)**

Book Hal as your Keynote Speaker and you're guaranteed to make your event highly enjoyable and unforgettable!

For more than a decade, **Hal Elrod** has been consistently rated as **the #1 Keynote Speaker** by meeting planners and attendees.

His unique style combines inspiring audiences with his unbelievable TRUE story, keeping them laughing hysterically with his high energy, stand-up comedy style delivery, and empowering them with actionable strategies to take their *RESULTS* to the *NEXT LEVEL*.

For more info visit **www.HalElrod.com**